LEADING and LEARNING

Fred Steven Brill

Foreword by Roland Barth

LEADING *and* LEARNING

Effective School Leadership Through Reflective Storytelling and Inquiry

Stenhouse Publishers   Portland, Maine

Stenhouse Publishers
www.stenhouse.com

Library of Congress Cataloging-in-Publication Data
Brill, Fred Steven, 1961–
  Leading and learning : effective school leadership through reflective storytelling and inquiry / Fred Steven Brill.
      p. cm.
  Includes bibliographical references and index.
    ISBN 978-1-57110-766-4 (alk. paper)
    1. School management and organization. 2. School principals--Professional relationships. 3. Educational leadership. I. Title.
    LB2805.B78 2008
    371.2--dc22

                          2008027446

Cover design, interior design, and typesetting by Designboy Creative Group

Manufactured in the United States of America on acid-free, recycled paper
14 13 12 11 10 09 08   9 8 7 6 5 4 3 2 1

To my very tolerant family,

Mimi,
Naya, Spencer, Ariana,
Cal, and Cella

There are many people who think they want to be matadors, only to find themselves in the ring with two thousand pounds of bull bearing down on them, and then discover that what they really wanted was to wear tight pants and hear the crowd roar.

 *Terry Pearce*

CONTENTS

Foreword ix

Acknowledgments xi

Introduction From Blind Passion to Professional Inquiry 1

PART I THE MANY HATS WORN BY THE SCHOOL LEADER 5

Chapter 1 The Reflective Storytelling Process: Illuminating the Path
from Novice to Expert Leadership 9

Chapter 2 The School Leader as Enforcer 27

Chapter 3 The School Leader as System Builder 37

Chapter 4 The School Leader as Equity Promoter 51

Chapter 5 The School Administrator as Instructional Leader 63

PART II SCHOOL LEADERSHIP: THE INTERSECTION OF DECISIONS,
VALUES, AND EMOTIONS 79

Chapter 6 Values in School Leadership: A Field of Pressure, Priorities,
and Principles 81

Chapter 7 The School Leader as Principal Decision Maker: A Field of Dreams,
Deliberations, and Derailments 99

Chapter 8 The School Leader as Human Pincushion: The Role of Emotions
in School Leadership 119

Chapter 9 Inhabiting the Role of School Leader: The Principal as Superhero 135

Afterword Lessons and Learnings from New School Leaders 151

References 157

Index 169

FOREWORD

"God so loved stories that he created mankind."

Eighteenth-century Rabbi Nachman had it right. Storytelling and mankind are inseparable. When you think about it, all of the world's most sacred writings are collections of stories. The Old Testament, New Testament, Koran, Talmud. What is a parable but a story with a teaching?

Alas, those who study this art form tell us that storytelling is dying. We used to sit around the kitchen table after supper and tell our stories. Now we don't even *eat* together!

In schools, of course, telling stories has no place in this era of suffocating accountability. Except in kindergarten! Storytelling is not rigorous, legitimate, research based, or testable. It's just "shooting the breeze."

Happily, this tidy little volume you are about to experience not only revives storytelling but also transforms it into a powerful form of leadership development.

If you put a quarter in the meter of any school leader, out will tumble a story. In fact, many stories… rich, moving, tedious, dull, funny, tragic stories. I used to gather late on Friday afternoons with a few other principals, and we would exchange events of the week. Most of these, like other practitioner stories, were descriptions of practice. "Let me tell you about the time I tried to fire this teacher. . . " And most have therefore been dismissed by academics and by principals themselves as "war stories." Fun, frivolous, and of little value to others or to the profession.

Actually, I think war stories have considerable value, else why would my principal buddies and I have engaged in them? They offer a means of bonding, entertainment, and a cathartic, emotional cleansing that enable us to put the week behind us so we can rejoin our families for the weekend. But war stories have precious little to offer to improve our practice.

It is only when the story about practice is accompanied by *analysis* of practice that the narrative is transformed from war story into craft knowledge. "Let me tell you about the time I tried to fire this teacher… and here's what I learned from the experience." We learn from experience only when we *reflect* on our experience.

I have long believed that if school practitioners would ever disclose even a small fraction of what they have learned during their careers in the schools of hard knocks—their craft knowledge about curriculum, parent involvement, discipline, staff development, scheduling—our schools would be transformed overnight.

Sadly, as a profession, we are not very good at disclosing to others what we have learned. And for good reasons: in a culture of competition, the underlying rule is, "the better you look, the worse I look." But, "the worse you look, the better I look." Starved for recognition, why would we want to give others our keys to the store?

And many educators believe they have little of value to offer. It is university researchers who harbor the treasure trove of wisdom. Thus, all too many practitioners have experienced and fear corrosive put-downs from their peers, like "Big deal, I've been doing that for years." Or, "What a trivial idea." So why share?

Others fail to disclose their craft knowledge for fear of revealing their blemishes. Who amongst us wants to appear weak and fumbling? As one principal told me, "I live under the burden of ascribed omniscience."

Even if there is a valuable story to tell and a wish to tell it, all too often disclosure of craft knowledge is greeted with glazed-over eyes. Unfortunately, in our field, the ability to listen is as primitive as the ability to share. Storytelling is dying for want of good listeners.

The newcomer to an organization is the most insightful observer of it. Yet for novices especially, sharing is seen as a violation of taboo: "You must teach here for three years before you can stand up in a faculty meeting and put forth your idea."

For all of these reasons and despite the best efforts of teacher leaders, principals, and staff developers, principals, like teachers, continue to live in their "self-contained classrooms." Their abundant craft knowledge languishes behind closed doors.

The gifts of this book to all of us in this beleaguered profession are many: by allowing, encouraging, and expecting principals to tell their stories, it demonstrates that principals *will* reveal. And it shows us just how to unlock both principal and story.

By elevating reflective storytelling to a systematic, habituated, and thoughtful behavior, it brings legitimacy—even urgency—to the stories of these school leaders. The intention of stories is not just to entertain. They can also teach us, touch us, and cause us to remember.

By unpacking and scrutinizing these stories alongside the reader, *Leading and Learning* develops helpful frames for analysis with which to mine the gold from the gravel. In doing so, the book reveals as much about the gritty essence of the job of the school principal as any volume I know.

There is one more contribution: the waters between school and university are muddy, disturbed places. Because Fred Brill is a citizen of both cultures, and because he has engaged these new principals as genuine collaborators, these words, like the insights, are "principal centered," fully approachable, and valuable to residents of each world. Indeed, the book represents a hopeful, all-too-rare example of fruitful cooperation between these two estranged worlds.

One thing we learn from these stories is that, contrary to the belief of many, principals are educable… if the conditions are right. A careful use of storytelling is clearly among the conditions that can promote profound levels of learning by leaders. It is clear from these stories that the ability and insight of principals coming into the profession is rich. This bodes well for our nation's schools. I only wish I had had access to this book during my own turbulent, troubled days as a school principal. They wouldn't have been so turbulent and troubled!

In short, dear reader, what you are about to encounter is a story about storytelling and storytellers. I couldn't agree more with Fred Brill that "There is much that can be learned by looking at stories told by new leaders."

Just what has been learned from the 246 stories of these new principals? Read on!

Roland S. Barth, May 2008

Acknowledgments

I would like to thank my parents, Ira and Julene Brill, for setting me up to take this extraordinary journey. I would also like to acknowledge my wife, Mimi Melodia, for riding beside me and hanging in there, along some backroads that read "curva peligrosa." My friends and mentors Camille Moore and Bob Blackburn have served as essential guides and cheerleaders throughout the sojourn! I need to begrudgingly offer my appreciation to Jill Duerr-Berrick, who implored me to code each and every narrative. "You'll never know if you're missing something," she taunted. And I would like to thank my running partner, Ken Epstein, who helped shape my thoughts, findings, and practice as we plodded along the trails of Mount Tamalpais. Norton Grubb has served as an extraordinary teacher and academic mentor, and his political rants and demands for linear thinking and the formation of a logical argument have left an indelible mark on my research and my practice. Equally, I would like to acknowledge Patricia Baquedano-Lopez for teaching me that the stories of new school leaders were important and worthy of academic inquiry. I owe a huge debt of gratitude to my colleagues and research partners, Lynda Tredway and Jeanette Hernandez, who contributed immensely to the thinking, planning, and development of many of the systems, codes, and protocols in this book. And I offer a heap of appreciation and respect for all members of the Principal Leadership Institute, whose commitment to creating an educational system of the highest quality for all children—and whose passion, thoughtfulness, and honest reflection—make up the stuff of this book. Thank heavens for Sandy Shaw, my supportive friend, surrogate mother, editor, and chiropractor, who has always watched my back. And finally, I want to thank Bill Varner for giving me a shot and offering sharp insight and direction in the creation of this book.

FROM BLIND PASSION TO PROFESSIONAL INQUIRY

Action without reflection is meaningless activity. Reflection without action is mere academia.

 *Peter Reason, 1998*

The seeds of this book began to sprout in the fertile grounds—the dirt, if you will—of my personal experience as a school leader. I served as an assistant principal for three years and then as a middle school principal for nine years. In reflecting on my own development as I struggled to learn the craft of educational leadership, I came to a very simple conclusion: it followed nothing less than a wild, erratic growth pattern, characterized by fits, sputters, stops, and periodic spurts of learning and development.

I did not have a professional learning community to provide the necessary support or structured opportunities that might have prompted me to reflect on and integrate my new experiences. I did not have the language or conceptual frameworks that would have allowed me to formulate a theoretical construct to inform my work as an instructional leader. I had no idea how other school administrators talked about their work, how they made decisions, how they chose which roles to play, or how they navigated the intense emotion that seemed to erupt whenever attempts of any kind were made to change school practice.

As a practitioner, rarely was I interested in—nor did I have the time to read—academic journals. Most scholarly books and articles seemed abstract, wordy, and not overly useful for refining or reforming my everyday practice. However, I recognized that thoughtful researchers had gone into the field to study and learn and then to share their findings. I knew there was much to learn from researchers. Although I understood the importance of using data to drive my decision making, I wondered about this disconnect: why the great divide between theory and practice for so many principals? Schön aptly encapsulated my concern about positioning myself too closely to the world of academia.

Universities are not devoted to the production and distribution of fundamental knowledge in general. They are institutions committed, for the most part, to a particular epistemology, a view of knowledge that fosters a selective inattention to practical competence and professional artistry. (1983, vii)

As a new principal, I was in desperate need of more information about the art and science of school leadership. I needed to do more than simply tell war stories to anyone who was willing to listen to my travails. I needed a means of framing the challenges I confronted daily. I needed guidance on how to develop an effective decision-making process. Most of all, I longed for a professional learning community that would prompt me to reflect on my practice in a supportive and structured manner.

As I entered graduate school at the University of California, Berkeley, I had the privilege and opportunity to help shape the structure of a new administrative induction program: the Leadership Support Program (LSP), an outgrowth of the Principal Leadership Institute. The Principal Leadership Institute is a program created by governor's legislation in 1999 in an effort to reinvigorate the preparation of urban educational leaders in the state of California. It is a fourteen-month (forty-unit) leadership preparation program at UC Berkeley that awards a master of arts in education and a preliminary administrative services credential.

The stories I use throughout this book were video- and audiotaped from school leaders who graduated from the Principal Leadership Institute, assumed positions as site administrators, and participated in UC Berkeley's Leadership Support Program. In the LSP, novice administrators meet one evening each month, from September through May. From the program's inception, my colleagues and I were committed to ensuring relevance in the learning activities we facilitated. With this perspective in mind, we adopted problem-based learning (Bridges 1992) as a foundation to explore the ways in which participants addressed challenges. We created structured opportunities for new school leaders to make meaning of their experiences and thoughtfully consider how they could apply their learnings to new challenges that emerged in their respective schools.

The monthly session of the Leadership Support Program began casually: participants tossed down briefcases, exchanged pleasantries, and worked through an evening meal. Before long, shoulders began to relax and brows unfurrowed. What happened next seemed born of necessity: stories literally poured out of these novice administrators, evoking tears and laughter as they replayed their most recent foibles and follies, as well as their successes.

By allowing new administrators to share a story with colleagues, site leaders forgo the persona of the superhero; they remove their capes and reveal the more authentic hand-wringing that takes place beneath the costume of the professional. Reflective storytelling was chosen as a primary tool in the LSP because the activity provides new leaders the opportunity for reflection, sensemaking, and theory building based on actual dilemmas confronted in the field. By looking at the aggregate of the narratives, by diving deep into the data set and unpacking the stories, unexpected patterns and findings emerge that provide a detailed picture of the internal landscape—the inner workings of novice school leaders.

The initial intent of this book was to explore how novice administrators make sense of, conceptualize, and talk about the many roles they play in a challenging, politically charged environment. But as new leaders analyzed their narratives over time, they offered rich reflections of the transformations that took place in their thinking, decision making, and action taking. They presented new ways that they conceptualized their work, and they even described positive feelings of efficacy as they reflected on the ways they were navigating the intense emotion they confronted in the field. Based on these collective observations and learnings, this text will explore how reflective storytelling and inquiry can prompt school leaders to

- better frame the dilemmas they confront;
- clarify their underlying values;
- determine an effective decision-making process;
- develop new theories and conceptions about their problem-solving;
- and increase their metacognitive thinking about their practice.

The prompts used to elicit the stories in this book were not topically prescriptive; participants were always given the opportunity to speak on any subject that they felt was important. Therefore, the transcribed narratives effectively capture the most salient and poignant issues upon which professional training and development should be based.

One of the greatest challenges I faced in writing this book was remembering which hat I was wearing. At one moment, I was capturing data to learn how new administrators make decisions, embody different roles, and navigate the intense emotion. In the next moment, I was designing protocols and analytical tools or facilitating groups to promote deep reflection and metacognitive processes. Then, of course, there was the endless writing, the search for the most eloquent turn of phrase to capture the essence of school leadership. Fortunately, I had 246 leadership narratives to draw upon that I had collected from new school leaders during a period of three years.

It has been an overwhelming and wildly rewarding endeavor to serve as a facilitator of professional development, a collaborative researcher, a storyteller, a listener, a creator of theories, a portraitist, a qualitative researcher, and, of course, a practitioner. I invite readers to learn from the stories—the slips, stumbles, and falls—shared by growth-oriented school leaders. More important, I urge practicing school leaders to create structured opportunities to engage in their own process of reflective storytelling within a professional learning community and to take charge of their own growth and development in becoming more thoughtful and effective leaders.

Part I

THE MANY HATS WORN BY THE SCHOOL LEADER

The school leader of today must play a panoply of roles, engage in a plethora of activities, and make a myriad of decisions to ensure student learning. The list of roles and responsibilities is vast and overwhelming. While we do know that principals with very different communication, management, and personality styles can be strong instructional leaders (Smith and Keith 1971), there has been little analysis of the ways new leaders talk about the various roles they play in striving to manage the responsibilities of their position and improve the teaching and learning in their schools.

Over a period of three years, I collected 246 narratives from novice school leaders enrolled in the University of California, Berkeley's Leadership Support Program. The stories were audio- or videotaped and transcribed for the benefit of researchers and practitioners alike, so that we could collectively understand the recurring themes, roles, and practices of new administrators. The beginning stages of this research were modeled after the work of Lawrence-Lightfoot:

First, we listen for repetitive refrains that are spoken (or appear) frequently and persistently, forming a collective expression of commonly held views. Second, we listen for resonant metaphors, poetic and symbolic expressions that reveal the way actors illuminate and experience their realities. Third, we listen for the themes expressed through cultural and institutional rituals that seem to be important to organizational continuity and coherence. Fourth, we use triangulation to weave together the threads of data converging from a variety of sources. And finally, we construct themes and reveal patterns among perspectives that are often experienced as contrasting and dissonant by the actors. (Lawrence-Lightfoot and Davis 1997, 193)

But which roles do new leaders most frequently play? Are these roles chosen or assigned? How do new leaders learn to play the roles they are uncomfortable playing? How do they learn to authentically inhabit the role of the school leader? By looking at the frequency of roles described in administrative narratives, one begins to get a picture not only of the concerns and challenges that new administrators face but also of their corresponding priorities and underlying values.

In September 2002, when we asked new leaders enrolled in the Leadership Support Program to identify the different roles they play, the list they compiled was vast and overwhelming: counselor, social worker, hand-holder/teacher supporter, problem-solver, listener, stress sponge, lunch server, traffic guard, police officer, nurse, mom, dad, enforcer, judge, disciplinarian/enforcer, moderator, peacemaker, coordinator, organizer, supervisor, mentor, observer, teacher, motivator, evaluator, ambassador, coach, student advocate, instructional leader, visionary, communicator, equity promoter, role model, parent liaison, researcher, investigator, custodian, test coordinator, scheduler, system challenger/system builder, accountant, fund-raiser, paper pusher, and manager.

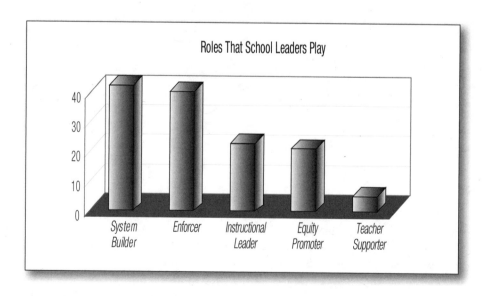

Participants were asked to consolidate this list and find larger baskets to hold these different roles. In the traditional academic paradigm, only the researcher designs the study, gathers the data, manages the project, draws conclusions, and builds new theories. However, engaging participants in a practice of collaborative inquiry afforded new leaders the opportunity to develop a common vocabulary and to identify and refine common roles and actions that characterized their practice. The process of coding encouraged participant researchers to move fluidly from theory to practice, from experience back to abstract reconceptualization.

In sum, new leaders were afforded ongoing opportunities to review their own narratives, develop their own set of codes, and create their own common language to better understand their practice. The most common roles that emerged in the 246 leadership stories were enforcer, system challenger, equity promoter, and instructional leader.

It is not at all surprising that one of the most common roles played by new school leaders is that of enforcer. New site administrators are regularly assigned the role of disciplinarian. However, if education is about the business of teaching and learning, why were only 15 percent of the narratives about actively and directly playing the role of instructional leader? Why did only 2 percent of the stories describe school leaders actively supporting teachers? Many of the narratives contained proclamations about the importance of serving as an instructional leader, but it appears that leaders were regularly compelled (or expected) to address the urgent before focusing on the important. As Karen M., a second-year elementary school principal, eloquently expresses:

> *I want to improve teaching and learning; that's what my whole life is about. At the same time when I first started as principal . . . I quickly discovered that I couldn't be about teaching and learning unless other things were in place. (April 2004)*

Although it is logical to expect that many new leaders would thirst to play the role of equity promoter, especially when observing or learning about an injustice or some form of discrimination toward a child, it was very surprising to find that the most common role new leaders described in their stories was that of system challenger. Even though school leaders complained of feeling overwhelmed, it appears that they were willing to move outside their prescribed job description to fill a gap or build a system to improve efficiency or effectiveness in the way business was conducted in their school communities.

In Chapter 1, I describe the critical and relentless role of the school leader, and I show how new leaders can manage their own professional development to move more deliberately along the continuum from novice to expert. I then show how storytelling—a natural and necessary activity—can serve as a tool for professional growth, especially when stories are shared with like-minded colleagues who understand the trials and tribulations of being a school leader. I describe in detail the structure of the reflective storytelling process, the primary activity used to prompt the sharing of meaningful and relevant narratives. I show the ways in which narratives were captured, and I share the various processes used to analyze the stories and to uncover common themes and patterns of practice.

In chapters 2 through 5, I highlight the common roles and activities that new leaders talk about in the stories they tell, with particular attention to the roles of enforcer, system challenger, equity promoter, and instructional leader. Each of these chapters includes relevant narratives shared by new school leaders that are unpacked and analyzed to uncover what can be learned from the decisions and actions described in the stories. Identifying, quantifying, and exploring the roles that new leaders play will be the starting point to understand how they can better prioritize and perform their work. At the end of each of these chapters, I offer probing questions that prospective and practicing school leaders might consider when reflecting on the ways in which they play (or might play) the different roles.

Chapter 1

THE REFLECTIVE STORYTELLING PROCESS:
Illuminating the Path from Novice to Expert Leadership

The Master gave his teaching in parables and stories—which his disciples listened to with pleasure—and occasional frustration, for they longed for something deeper. The Master was unmoved. To all their objections he would say, "You have yet to understand, my dears, that the shortest distance between a human being and Truth is a story."

Anthony DeMello, 1985

Novice school leaders tend to be passionate individuals who are hungry to learn and grow and improve their practice. They understand that education is crucial for the students they serve, but also that it is essential for their own survival as a school leader. Although many a leader would relish the opportunity to reflect on a prickly decision or contemplate how to work through a complex personnel issue, different constituents and stakeholders expect leaders to have the *right* answers and to take *appropriate* actions immediately and decisively. Implement! Execute! Decide! But how and when do school administrators make sense of the many challenges they face? How do they become more effective in the art and science of school leadership?

Novice administrators regularly talk of being overwhelmed by the relentlessness of their work; they express uneasiness with the ambiguity of the roles they are expected to play. They struggle to find meaning and to create coherence and clarity in their work.

Being new to a leadership position, being new to a school site, or being unclear about roles, responsibilities, and expectations can be highly stress inducing. It takes time and experience to comfortably assume the identity of a school leader. Before we explore how reflective storytelling might be used as a tool for professional growth and development, it is important to understand why the role of the school leader is so important to a school's success.

THE CRITICAL AND RELENTLESS ROLE
OF THE SCHOOL LEADER

Whenever one finds an effective school, there exists an effective principal as its leader.

—Daisy Gonzalez, 1997

A 2004 report commissioned by the Wallace Foundation found that leadership ranked second only to teaching in improving student achievement (Leithwood, Anderson, and Wahlstrom 2004). Although successful school leaders spend significant time at the intersection of teaching and learning, they are also responsible for the operational management of the school, community relations, and culture building. At one moment, they may be putting a Band-Aid on a child's knee; the next moment, they might be working with an angry parent whose child was suspended for fighting. One day, they are facilitating the professional development on rubric development for teachers; the next day, they are convening a school site council to determine the best use of Title I funds. Educational leaders are charged with setting the tone, crafting the vision, and making good decisions to create a clean, safe, and healthy learning environment for every member of the school community.

Indeed, the principalship is one of the most exciting and rewarding roles in the world of education. It is the position at the epicenter of school reform and site-level decision making. A strong principal cultivates an effective learning community for students, teachers, and parents, and is able to develop strong relationships with individuals across stakeholder groups. The effective principal is the conduit, the connection, the spark, the stick, the carrot, the architect, and the builder responsible for ensuring that effective teaching and learning is taking place for every student in every classroom throughout the school. But can school leaders really meet the needs, expectations, and mandates of all stakeholders? Bolman and Deal question the implied notion of school leader as superhero:

> *We have certainly tried to make organizations better… The most basic change strategy is to change management and leadership. Modern mythology promises that organizations will work splendidly if they are well managed. (1997, 8)*

The position of school principal requires an ability to recognize and understand the root causes of the challenges emerging in the field. It necessitates continual reprioritization and alignment of scarce resources. In addition, the work must be done beneath the stage lights, where any decisions and actions, signs of tentativeness, and missteps or miscommunications are witnessed and judged by a wide swath of stakeholders. Indeed, impeccable judgment is expected at most every turn. Ours has become an extremely litigious culture, and the principal is expected to serve thoughtfully without ever breaking a sweat, decide without showing any sign of angst or uncertainty, and resolve so that all parties feel listened to and validated. Unfortunately, like any baseball manager who does not get immediate and favorable outcomes, the school leader is subject to replacement at the end of the season.

The responsibilities, conflicting expectations, time demands, stressors, and challenges associated with administrative positions often make such jobs highly undesirable. In his exploration of why teachers are unwilling to move into administration, Duane Moore found that the top three reasons for not becoming a principal were "increased time commitments, the influence of outside groups, and too much bureaucratic paperwork" (1999). The principal is getting pushed further and further away from the business of teaching and learning. One school leader described the sense of being overwhelmed by the competing demands:

> *And then I get to my office this afternoon, and I have papers all over the place. You can always tell what kind of state my work life is in because when it's really, really busy, there's just papers falling off the desk and under the desk. And you know, I keep putting things into my in-basket; my in-basket now is like this [holds hands about three feet apart]. And I just felt so frazzled because I knew I had to get here by five, and I've usually been staying until eight o'clock every night, so I was like, "Crap, I don't have time." (Gretchen C., September 2002)*

In a typical workday, few school leaders are afforded the opportunity to reflect on their practice, the decisions they make, or the actions they take. Yet, regular reflection on practice is imperative for professional growth and development. School leaders are calling for structured opportunities to serve as coresearchers and co-learners who base their learning on actual challenges confronted in the field. Although the job of school leader is not for everyone, it is clear that—with the proper training and support—administrators can become more effective, resilient, reflective, deliberate, principle-based leaders. New leaders can learn to choose where they allocate their time and other precious resources, and how they might work more effectively to make decisions and improve student learning.

ADULT LEARNING THEORY

School leaders must persistently exhibit, model, and celebrate lifelong learning themselves... If [students] see adults who are constantly asking questions, reading, sharing good ideas, and posing and solving problems, so will they.

—Roland Barth in DuFour, Eaker, and DuFour, 2005

Adult learning theory suggests that professionals learn not only from their own practice, which is a trial-and-error type of learning, but also from interactions—formal and informal conversations—with other professionals (Bransford, Brown, and Cocking 2000). When systems and protocols are embedded within a professional learning community, there are more likely to be higher levels of achievement, more positive relationships, and psychologically healthier group members than might be found in individual learning situations (Brown and Campione 1996).

One fact is clear from looking at the research on professional development: learning and reflection do not happen readily in isolation. Learning is a social activity, and it comes largely from our participation in daily life. *Communities of practice* are everywhere (Lave and Wenger 1991); they emerge in social and professional settings, and they fill an inherent need for struggling individuals to make sense of their challenges. One new school leader explained:

> *We've got to learn from each other's mistakes. I'm not going to live long enough to make them all myself. (Sally B., October 2003)*

In addition to managing their own internal change process, school leaders are responsible for moving school reform efforts forward. But change is hard, in individuals and within organizations. The school leader will be expected to tend to the emotional responses from the teachers and support staff who are expected to implement and adopt new practices and strategies.

> *One of the most damaging myths that aspiring school administrators often learn is that the change process, if managed well, will proceed smoothly. That myth amounts to little more than a cruel hoax, an illusion that encourages educators to view problems and conflict as evidence of mistakes or mismanaged process rather than as the inevitable byproducts of serious reform. (DuFour and Eaker 1998, 49)*

Indeed, the school leader must manage dissension and opposition, setbacks, and unintended consequences. Although it is sometimes excruciatingly challenging, school leaders also must maintain an unshakable belief that all human beings, *including adults,* can continually learn and grow.

If an inquiry stance is maintained, any challenges, failures, and setbacks can become clear indicators of the need to adjust, refine, or improve a particular process. In his book *How People Change,* Allen Wheelis argues that, although "character has a forward propulsion that tends to carry it unaltered into the future, suffering can lead to insight, will, action, and ultimately *change*" (1973, 101). Those engaged in collaborative inquiry will make meaning of past experiences and return to the field to test their new theories and actions in an ongoing cycle of experimentation and learning. This is a process that effective school leaders regularly engage in and facilitate.

THE PROFESSIONAL LEARNING COMMUNITY: A SPACE FOR REFLECTIVE STORYTELLING

> *If there is anything that the research community agrees on, it is this: The right kind of continuous, structured… collaboration improves the quality of teaching and pays big, often immediate, dividends in student learning and professional morale in virtually any setting.*
>
> —*Richard DuFour, Robert Eaker, and Rebecca DuFour, 2005*

New school leaders are expected to burst forth from the cloistered phone booth of an administrative credentialing program, take to the air, and effectively meet the needs of all students, teachers, parents, and higher-level administrators. Unfortunately, leadership development programs are not generally structured or organized in such a way that prospective leaders are prepared to address the challenges they will face and the various roles they will be expected to play in the school setting. Classroom learning for professionals is inclined toward the theoretical rather than the practical.

Sadly, "collaboration is not natural or common in the traditional school environment. For generations, teachers characteristically closed the classroom door behind them and acted as independent monarchs of their own domains, expecting neither oversight nor support from colleagues" (Blankenstein 2004, 137). It is tragic that schools become environments in which teachers engage in a form of *parallel play*. Child psychologists describe this behavior in preschoolers as when similar activities take place in different corners of a sandbox, with nary a word of interaction flowing between the children. In school environments, those who have participated in committees to improve one area of the school typically have not met with much success in making a difference or even having their voices heard. One new leader offered his favorite quote when the subject of professional collaboration was being discussed: "A committee is a cul-de-sac down which ideas are lured and then quietly strangled" (James S., February 2003; quote from Sir Barnett Cocks, former British Clerk of the House of Commons). Clearly, a lot of work needs to be done to get educators to learn, understand, and experience the value of participating in a professional learning community.

Professional learning communities (PLCs) are intended to do much more than provide emotional support and encouragement. Under the proper conditions, participants will begin to take risks and share genuine concerns as they move along the continuum from novice to expert. Structured opportunities for reflective storytelling can ensure relevance and immediacy, as group members hold one another responsible for examining and acquiring essential bodies of skills and knowledge (DuFour and Eaker 1998). With proper training, colleagues can learn to prod one another toward growth and development. Challenging situations presented in the form of leadership stories can provide rich fodder for collaborative inquiry, reflection, and professional learning.

In the world of education, professional learning communities have become all the rage. Workshops are held around the country to promote the creation of collaborative structures focused on the improvement of student learning. DuFour and Eaker (1998) describe the critical components of a professional learning community: participants develop a shared mission, vision, and values; they engage in collective inquiry, which includes public reflection and the building of a shared meaning; they maintain an action orientation, promoting experimentation and a focus on continual improvement; and, finally, they maintain a strong outcomes orientation that places a high value on results rather than intentions. The four guiding questions that are intended to frame the work of a professional learning community (Dufour, Eaker, and DuFour 2005, 15) are:

- What is it we want all students to learn?
- How will we know when each student has mastered the essential learning?
- How will we respond if a student experiences initial difficulty in learning?
- How will we deepen the learning for students who have already mastered essential knowledge and skills?

It is no wonder that PLCs are gaining traction in public and private organizations. Professional learning communities can meet so many basic human needs: the need for a sense of belonging and acceptance, the need for esteem based on learning and growth, the need to serve a higher moral purpose, and the need for meaning in our work and our lives. If this sounds vaguely familiar, it is because it calls to mind Maslow (1943) and his hierarchy of needs. The lower level of Maslow's pyramid contains our basic human needs (physiological requirements such as oxygen, food, and water). The next levels are safety; love, acceptance, and belonging; and esteem in the community. The apex of the pyramid, the highest form of human development, is the need for self-actualization. Maslow argued that the only reason individuals would not move toward self-actualization is because of hindrances placed in their way by society. Sadly, educational organizations often fit neatly into this category. DuFour and Eaker describe the role that professional learning communities can play in meeting these higher human needs:

> *Above all else, there is a basic human desire to live a life of meaning, to serve a higher purpose, to make a difference in the world… The professional learning community sets out to restore that belief by creating a community of caring and mutual concern… When educators connect with one another, they can accomplish far more collectively than they could ever hope to accomplish individually… Educators hunger for evidence that they are successful in their work, that they are part of a significant collective endeavor, and that their efforts are making a difference in the lives of their students. (1998, 281–282)*

THE ROLE OF SCHOOL LEADER IN A PROFESSIONAL LEARNING COMMUNITY

The future of leadership must be embedded in the hearts and minds of the many, and not rest on the shoulders of the heroic few.

—*Alan Blankenstein, 2004*

What is the role of the school leader in cultivating professional learning communities? Where and how do school leaders get to reflect on their own craft? If PLCs are primarily about teachers collaboratively engaging in the improvement of the teaching and learning activities that take place in their classrooms, what is the role of the school leader in this process?

Much has been written about the "loose coupling" that exists in school organizations (Meyer and Rowan 1977; Tyack and Cuban 1995). Regardless of administrative intentions, desires, suggestions, or expectations, it can be very challenging to influence teacher practice. School leaders are not direct service providers. Rather, the teachers are responsible for student learning, and a classroom with a closed door has proven to be a safe haven for students and teachers to do what they have always done and to resist the latest school reform effort. For school leaders to achieve a desired outcome of improved student learning, they first must figure out how to influence teacher actions in the classroom. At the same time, they must efficiently tend to the various operational responsibilities and institutional expectations that are part of the position.

Building on the four guiding questions asked by DuFour, Eaker, and DuFour (2005), I propose four questions that must be continually addressed within a professional learning community of school leaders:

- What is it we want all teachers to know and be able to do?

- How will we know when each teacher has mastered the essential learning and is actively using the agreed-on tools and strategies?

- How will we respond if a teacher experiences initial difficulty in learning or actively resists implementation?

- How will we cultivate leadership capacity and opportunity for those teachers who have already mastered essential knowledge and skills?

School administrators cannot improve a school and increase student learning on their own. A primary mission for all educators is to help students understand that their education is not about their parents or their teachers or their principal—rather, it is for their own benefit. It is intended to increase their opportunities for success in college or the workplace. Likewise, a primary charge of the school leader is to help teachers understand that collaborative processes and active engagement in a professional learning community are not about the principal, the district, the state, or the federal government. These are simply the best ways we know to do business. Over time, as these practices become systemic, the principal becomes less visible and works behind the scenes to ensure that teachers have the necessary support and resources to participate fully and deeply in a professional learning community; the notion of *distributed leadership* becomes a reality rather than a buzzword. Professional learning communities can provide the structures to engage in collaborative inquiry for the purpose of improving instructional practice and determining the necessary actions that must be taken to ensure that all students are learning.

The role of the school principal is one of the loneliest and most challenging positions in the field of education. School leaders must seek out or create their own PLCs, so that they—like students and teachers—continually engage in reflective practices with colleagues who are interested in growing and improving their practice. Professional learning communities are all about translating theory into practice, learning into action. DuFour, Eaker, and DuFour recommend that educators "use transformation in thought, word, and deed as the standard against which you assess the quality of your own learning and that of others in the school community" (2005, 173).

THE POWER OF LANGUAGE, THE POWER OF STORY

Your beliefs become your thoughts. Your thoughts become your words. Your words become your actions. Your actions become your habits. Your habits become your values. Your values become your destiny.

—*Mahatma Gandhi, 1869–1948*

The need to communicate and connect with those who understand is profound. Even without the formal structures of a professional learning community, new leaders often are drawn to one another for mutual support and the opportunity to share their latest war stories. Great catharsis can be achieved merely by opening the floodgates and allowing emotionally charged stories and anecdotes to spill forth. Through reflective storytelling, new leaders can begin the (sometimes painful) process of self-reflection. As one new leader confessed, "In administration, the real you can't help but come out; the way you handle difficult situations makes you naked in front of the whole school community" (Frank S., March 2004). Reflective storytelling is not about providing a platform for self-flagellation; the process is intended to create the space for thoughtful deliberation that leads to professional growth. With structured protocols in place, storytelling can become more focused and relevant, and it can inform the practice of reflective school leaders.

The need to understand the complexities of school leadership is deep and far-reaching. School leaders are influenced by past experiences, personality characteristics, and their ability to learn and adapt; novice leaders also must find a way to comprehend the challenges they are confronting in the field. Storytelling can function as a means to make sense of new experiences. One school leader described his jarring entrance into the world of educational administration:

> **"** *Before I became a principal, I believed I was absolutely prepared for the role. As a teacher-leader, I was given enormous responsibility, training, and coaching. I was fairly successful, and I believed the transition would be seamless. About three months into the job, I hadn't slept through a single night without dreaming about my work, leaving myself voice mails, and taking notes in the middle of the night about what I did wrong and what I needed to do first thing in the morning. I called up my mentor and asked her, "Why didn't you ever tell me how hard it would be? Why didn't you warn me?" And she just laughed and laughed. (Brett F., November 2002)* **"**

In addition to serving as a means to communicate life events, storytelling can be a platform for expressing beliefs and personal values. Narratives not only arise from experience, they also shape perceptions of experience. Storytelling helps us explain, rationalize, and clarify our personal experiences (Labov and Waletzky 1967). Folklore, literary analysis, psychology, and sociolinguistics offer overlapping theoretical frames that shed light on the ways that stories can be used as a tool to communicate or construct our personal identity, to learn, to help us make sense of the way the world works, and to illuminate where and how we are situated in our workplace.

Personal narratives shared by new school leaders offer a firsthand account of how other administrators adopt the language of the profession and how they are socialized into their role within the school community. Baquedano-Lopez describes this process of identity formation:

In everyday life, and across the lifespan, we assume moral stances as we communicate with people and assess ideas or events. Language allows us to negotiate notions of morality and it provides a medium through which moral understanding of lives and events, our orientation in the world as individuals and as part of a collectivity are constructed, maintained and transformed. (1998, 109)

The difficulty of learning to speak the "language of the school leader" is often shared in the stories told by novice school leaders as they struggle to find agency and identity in their new roles. Participation in a new culture is not merely about learning *from* the talk; rather, it is about learning *to* talk with the appropriate nuance, emotion, and grammar of the school leader (Lave and Wenger 1991). Effective use of language can influence the practices and corresponding outcomes of new school leaders.

If language is the vessel through which meaning is transported (March 1994), it is no wonder that reflective storytelling can provide entertainment, relevance, and insight to the struggling administrator. New school leaders need to make sense of their new experiences. They need to make meaning of the roles they are playing and the decisions they are making, and storytelling can effectively meet such needs. As John Searle, professor of philosophy, asserts: "Words shape our thinking. Thinking shapes our reality" (2004). Deveare Smith, a qualitative researcher/performance artist, articulates her appreciation for the power that stories possess to shape our perceptions of reality:

I had never thought that our reality was so dependent on narratives… it may be that we need narratives to create a certain fiction… The creation of language is the creation of a fiction. The minute we speak, we are in that fiction. It's a fiction designed, we hope, to reveal a truth. There is no "pure" language. The only "pure language" is the initial sounds of a baby… We are linguistic animals. At the very least language is currency as we create "reality." (2000, 293)

Administrators learn very quickly that the language they use is vitally important and deeply considered by the various stakeholders in the school community. Indeed, words and stories not only convey thoughts, feelings, and perceptions, they also serve to shape our conceptions of the world. Language and the development of a common vocabulary can be very powerful tools in a school leader's arsenal.

THEORY DEVELOPMENT THROUGH STORYTELLING

To gain a new level of insight into personal behavior, the reflective practitioner assumes a dual stance, being, on one hand, the actor in a drama and, on the other hand, the critic who sits in the audience watching and analyzing the performance.

—Karen Osterman and Robert Kottkamp, 1993

By participating in a structured process of storytelling and analyzing shared narratives, new leaders are better able to integrate their new experiences, reflect deeply on their decisions, and identify outcomes connected to their actions. In the field of psychology, analysts work with clients to make formal interpretations of the stories they are told; they sift through the facts presented in search of *narrative truth* as a means to shift perceptions of past experiences and shape the possibility for future behavior. In the school setting, exposure to colleagues' multiple theories of action can enable participants to become more aware that their own practice is theory laden, and from such awareness comes the possibility of alternative plans for how one might operate in the field.

Reflective storytelling and narrative analysis are highly iterative processes that create the space for school leaders to describe the challenges they face and to consider possible decisions and actions. When colleagues ask probing questions, leaders have the opportunity to further unpack their actions and intentions and to explain how they made decisions, why they made such decisions, and how they felt throughout the process. The reflective storytelling process also supports the development of metacognitive practices and skills in emotional intelligence (Goleman 1995). Indeed, storytelling serves to bridge the great divide between theory and practice (see Figure 1.1).

Figure 1.1

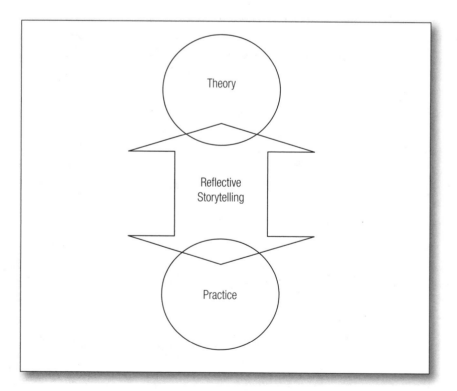

Reflective practitioners must find structured opportunities to consider their own experiences and corresponding theories of action, but sometimes they require a gentle nudge (or even a sharp elbow) from colleagues to consider alternative theories and frameworks. When theories of action are on the table in a professional learning community, they are subject to public questioning and scrutiny. Following the appropriate protocols, new leaders can engage in a rich process of collegial sensemaking. Such reflective activities encourage all members of a learning community to see how their decisions and actions are based on theories that can (and should) be adapted and adjusted continually as new information and understanding emerges. Brown and Campione assert:

> *Audiences demand coherence, push for higher levels of understanding, require satisfactory explanations, request clarification of obscure points, and so on. The sense of audience is not imaginary, but palpable and real... In time, reflective activities become internalized as auto-criticism and self-reflective thought. (1996, 294)*

A PARADIGM SHIFT IN PROFESSIONAL DEVELOPMENT

The use of storytelling as a form of adult learning is a profound shift in the way school leaders traditionally have engaged in professional development. Although it is not unusual for a professional developer to allow participants a few minutes to check in with table partners at the start of a meeting, this is often where storytelling ends. In the traditional model, a professional developer or professor dictates to his students a particular subject or competency to be mastered. It is assumed that professional growth will come in the form of neatly packaged research studies, prescribed competencies, and learning modules harvested from academic literature. This is similar to the way that many school reforms and curricular shifts have been handed down from central offices and from state and federal "educrats":

> *Recent legislated attempts at school reform share many similarities with older curricular change efforts. Legislators developed reform policies, mandates and programs for schools. They distributed these to educators through memos, lengthy documents, and state department of education emissaries who conducted information sessions indistinguishable in process from those used in curricular change attempts. External experts defined and solved the problem; others then delivered the answer for implementation. Again, they emphasized information transfer... The result has been the same: It didn't work! (Osterman and Kottkamp 1993, 3–4)*

It is tragic that storytelling often has been seen as a frivolous, unproductive activity; the act of sharing not only facilitates connection and caring among colleagues, it also promotes a process of sensemaking and the reconceptualization of practice. Storytelling without reflection can present as a form of entertainment, but reflective storytelling can serve as a springboard for professional development. Growth-oriented leaders relish the opportunity to contemplate their craft and to thoughtfully consider the many decisions they have made and have yet to make, without performing under the all-too-bright lights of school leadership.

For reflective storytelling to make its way into the world of professional development, it will need to face certain challenges. Professional developers may feel uncomfortable giving up precious time for storytelling. Stories are so elusive, fleeting, and ethereal. In addition, it sometimes seems as though new leaders cannot be trusted to construct their own knowledge. In 1938, John Dewey exposed the vital connection between experience and learning. The use of storytelling requires a trust that professionals, working in teams, can and will grab hold of opportunities to tease out a deeper understanding of the ways in which their words and actions may have been received and perceived.

The passion for story often presents as a primordial need and does not disappear when we slip into the costume of the professional. Human beings have an innate desire to learn with and from others, to be inspired, and to share. When asked if participating in such reflective activities was of value, one new elementary school principal explained, "It's the loneliest job in the world, and it seems like you guys are the only ones who understand my stories and help me understand… of course I'm going to keep coming" (Gretchen C., May 2003).

The Reflective Storytelling Process

In the reflective storytelling process, new administrators come together in a professional learning community that has clearly defined norms and protocols. Some larger school districts offer such professional development every two weeks, but other principals have organized their own collaborative networks of principals who work in the same county or region and meet on a monthly basis, using a less formal structure.

Participants are asked to work in pairs or triads, and they take turns sharing a story. Ten to fifteen minutes are generally allotted for this portion of the protocol. Over time, it is helpful to maintain the same critical friendship groups to build trust and understanding of context and ongoing challenges. For obvious reasons, norms of confidentiality are reinforced at every session. Participants are given prompts that are designed to elicit stories of an account in which they or some member of the school community experienced (or is experiencing) a form of emotional distress. The theory is that, when individuals experience some kind of emotional quandary, they are more receptive to feedback—they are more eager to understand the nuances of the situation and to think critically about what got them into such a stressful situation. The prompts provide an opening for new leaders to explore the triggers to intense emotion and analyze the ways in which they navigate (or might navigate) the challenges with which they are confronted.

In my role as both cofacilitator and researcher for the Leadership Support Program, I collected approximately six narratives from each participant over a period of three years. During the first year of the program, my colleagues and I chose to collect only three sets of narratives during September, October, and November. The stories themselves served as a tool for professional growth, but the collection of narratives represented a rich data set that could be mined to better understand the thinking and decision-making processes of novice administrators. In 2003 and 2004, many more narratives were audio- or videotaped and transcribed, excluding equipment failures or when new leaders told us that they simply did not want to be recorded. Names of participants, schools, and districts have been changed or eliminated to protect confidentiality.

Prompts for Reflective Storytelling

- Describe the biggest goal or challenge you are facing this year.

- What have you done in the school setting that reflects (or challenges) your vision and values?

- What decisions have you made that were considered daring by yourself or others?

- What is the hardest thing (or the best thing) that happened to you during the last week?

- Tell a story in which you were expected to play a role you were uncomfortable playing.

- Tell a story in which a decision you made was opposed by at least one stakeholder (parent, student, teacher, union representative, district office administrator).

- Describe a situation in which you felt misunderstood or misrepresented.

- Tell a story about a policy you implemented that was met with resistance.

- Tell about an "aha" that you have experienced so far this year.

- Tell a story about how you have negotiated the state and federal accountability agenda and corresponding communications with your staff and/or community.

- Describe a situation in which you dealt with intense emotion.

- Describe a difficult or unpalatable decision you had to make, and describe the decision-making process you used.

- Tell a story that showcases the heroes, villains, or fools in your school.

- Tell a story about a time you were confronted with a situation for which you were unprepared.

- Describe a decision you had to make that called into question your philosophy and guiding principles.

Although there can be tremendous value in simply sharing and hearing a story, the process becomes much richer when reflective questions are used to deepen understanding. (New leaders quickly learn that friends and family can't always appreciate or understand the complexity of the challenges they bring home each night.) After the storytelling portion of the process, listeners pose variations of the following reflective questions to elicit further contemplation of choices, roles, and actions. The active listeners are reminded to refrain from delving into their own similar quandaries; instead, they are expected to offer clarifying and probing questions to bring out the depth in the story and expose motivations, intentions, values, and desired outcomes. It is also helpful to push for elaboration of the decision-making processes that were used and the involvement (or exclusion) of various stakeholders.

Reflective Questions

- Why did you choose to tell this particular story?

- What was the primary challenge you faced?

- What precipitated this particular problem/dilemma?

- What were your intended outcomes when you became involved in the situation?

- How did you settle on these outcomes?

- How did you go about resolving the situation?

- What process did you use to make your key decisions or choose a particular course of action?

- Who, if anyone, did you involve in your decision-making process?

- Who did you exclude from your decision-making process? Why?

- Were you satisfied with the results of your actions?

- What emotions did you experience throughout the situation?

- Did these emotions color the way in which you responded, either positively or negatively? Explain.

- How would different members of the school community describe the way you handled yourself and the situation?

- If you had to do it all over again, would you respond differently to the situation?

REFLECTION THROUGH NARRATIVE ANALYSIS

Tremendous value often exists in simply sharing and hearing a story; however, to make storytelling even more powerful and provocative, it can be especially useful to videotape, audiotape, and transcribe narratives. This captures the fleeting nature of storytelling by turning the narratives into material artifacts. Work on tangible artifacts is one common feature of many professional learning communities (Little 2002). It is much easier to review and analyze something that is material and concrete through a variety of analytical lenses.

When new leaders observe how they present themselves or have an opportunity to read their own narratives, the experience can be rather shocking and disconcerting. First, the broken language and faulty grammar typical of casual conversation do not always come across well in print. Next, repetitive refrains ("you know?") can distract from the core message. More significantly, the ways in which new leaders sometimes talk about their work with children and adults can be perceived as controlling, disrespectful, and filled with generalizations. Taking the time to dissect the words and phrases we use, and their corresponding effect on different audiences, is but one protocol that can help new leaders better understand the profound power of their language.

Engaging in a process of narrative analysis can be compared to the work of an archeologist; we must carefully dig and dust off the key artifacts embedded in each story. Each word, phrase, or metaphor can offer clues about emotional content, guiding principles, and stakeholder expectations. The grammar, cadence, and structure of the story line can expose the way new leaders actively reflect on the challenges and decisions they are wrestling with in the field.

Making sense of an experience or story involves a search for themes and patterns, a process of chunking and sorting. In the traditional academic paradigm, the researcher designs the study, gathers the data, manages the project, draws conclusions, and builds new theories. However, engaging in a collaborative process of narrative analysis with like-minded colleagues affords new leaders the opportunity to study common actions and decision-making processes and to refine conceptual theories that characterize the practice of school leadership.

It is important to note that a marked difference often exists in the type of interaction that emerges immediately after an audio or video recorder is turned off; some of the more powerful and relevant debriefing takes place in these moments. The informal conversation, commiseration, and problem-solving become more animated and seem to spring to life when stories are no longer being recorded. A structured process of storytelling can elicit reflection and learning, but it is important to remember that no one can control when or how learning takes place.

CHANGES IN PRACTICE

The study of personal and professional narratives is not the most precise science; however, much can be learned from studying the patterns of practice that emerge during a micro and macro analysis of leadership stories. Peter Reason readily acknowledges the shortcomings of such qualitative methodology, yet he supports continued work in this area of academic exploration:

> There are no procedures that will guarantee valid knowing, or accuracy, or truth. There are simply human beings in a certain place and time, working away, more or less honestly, more or less systematically, more or less collaboratively, more or less self-awarely to seize the opportunities of their lives, solve the problems which beset them, and to understand the things that intrigue them. (1988, 231)

Many of the stories shared by new school leaders illuminate the quandaries and unsolvable dilemmas they face, while other tales highlight foolish or impulsive actions taken. In mining these narratives, it is important to remember that there are sometimes profound differences in what people say, what people do, and what people say they do. Nonetheless, engaging in reflective storytelling can influence the ways in which new leaders think, speak, and act.

The stories captured through the reflective storytelling process and included in this book provide a treasure trove of anecdotes that collectively represent the ways in which new school leaders reflect on their decisions and actions, conceptualize their practice, make meaning, and develop metacognitive skills.

Reflective Questions for Prospective and Practicing School Leaders

- What form of professional development do you find most useful and informative? What form is least useful and informative?

- What kinds of professional learning are most enjoyable? What kinds are least enjoyable?

- Do you have structured opportunities to make sense of your professional practice and to learn from and with your colleagues?

- How can you create or improve collaborative opportunities that will prompt individual and organizational learning?

- What is your primary purpose as a school leader? How closely aligned are your thoughts, words, and actions to your purpose?

- Are there individuals or stakeholder groups with whom you regularly experience conflict?

- Do you have a colleague or mentor with whom you can regularly share your professional challenges and wonderings?

- Are there common themes or patterns in the kinds of stories you tell?

- Have you established structured and regular times to reflect on your decisions and actions? What does this entail?

- What kinds of issues are you most likely to take on as a challenge in your professional world?

- How does your use of language in your role as a school leader differ from how you talk about your practice in a professional learning community among colleagues?

- How frequently do you slow down (or extract yourself) from a challenging situation and thoughtfully consider or map out the next steps?

❧ What could you do differently to ensure more regular on-the-job reflection?

❧ What actions have you taken in your school community to create a sense of urgency around a particular challenge?

❧ Have you created the conditions in your school to promote collaboration and professional learning communities?

❧ Is there a common understanding of the goals, expectations, and values in your school community? Why or why not?

Chapter 2

THE SCHOOL LEADER AS ENFORCER

The faculty comes from a place of trying to see the criminal in the student. They're looking for what the kid's doing wrong rather than what the kid's doing right.

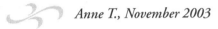

Anne T., November 2003

Most new school leaders enter school administration directly from the classroom, where they have served successfully as master teachers. They are quickly nudged out of the nest and expected to fly gracefully into a world of discipline and accountability, with very little training or preparation. New leaders can unfurl their wings and prove that they are up to the challenging task of educational leadership by assuming roles such as dean, vice principal, or assistant principal. Although principals are now expected to serve primarily as instructional leaders, it is ironic that the enforcer roles are often the gateway to the principalship.

Holding students and other members of the school community accountable for adhering to the rules and unwritten expectations of the institution can consume a considerable amount of administrative time. Although leadership preparation programs are beginning to emphasize the importance of instructional leadership, learning how to "do discipline" often fails to make it into the core curriculum.

The relatively recent popularity of standardized testing has helped to reinforce the belief that the primary role of the teacher and the school is to impart cognitive skills. Mastering course material, however, is only one aspect of schooling. Too often ignored is the equally important role of socialization... At the same time that teacher discipline helps control the learning environment and thus facilitates instruction, it also serves an important role in socialization... The moral authority of school discipline is critical in fostering students' ability to learn socially appropriate behaviors and values so they can become healthy individuals and productive citizens. (Arum 2003, 186)

Much can be learned by listening to stories told by new school leaders. Twenty-two percent of the stories told by the novice leaders enrolled in the Leadership Support Program depicted them playing the role of the *enforcer*. Generally, these stories were about disciplining students; however, many of the stories also were about enforcing rules and policies that were violated by teachers and support staff in the school.

Novice school leaders are often responsible for working with those students who are sent out of class for misbehavior. They are also expected to address any problems that arise in the schoolyard before school, at lunch, and after school. New leaders regularly describe themselves as being shoehorned into the role of enforcer, and they often experience internal angst as they learn the language and behaviors of the position. Playing the role of enforcer involves developing a safe and productive learning environment, and creating and enforcing systems and structures so that individuals and groups can work and learn efficiently and effectively. So, how do new leaders make this position meaningful? How do they learn to inhabit this necessary, but often uncomfortable, role?

Cultural institutions—including schools—regularly objectify, organize, classify, exclude, evaluate, and subjugate individuals into "docile bodies" (Foucault 1977), and language is a common tool that has been used to socialize both students and administrators into highly prescribed roles. When educators accept a new position within a traditional public school system, a peculiar dichotomy can emerge. New leaders, especially those who work in urban school districts, tend to be highly committed to equity and the education of all children; yet, in order to ensure a safe environment, they often are charged with suspending and expelling students (for the greater good) and denying those children who may be most in need of an education.

Foucault (1977), in his study of the culture of prisons, argued that narratives are shaped by the institutions in which the storytellers reside. This notion was depicted clearly in the Stanford Prison Study (Zimbardo 1971), in which college students were asked to play the roles of prisoners and prison guards; the experiment had to be ended early because the students who were playing prison guards became too aggressive and abusive in their assigned roles. They quickly adopted the talk and the walk of prison guards with tremendous zeal. Similarly, many new administrators see themselves as lifting students up and out of the culture of poverty—providing opportunity and power to the disenfranchised—while they unwittingly perpetuate the language of the oppressor.

Dozens of stories shared by new school leaders convey the struggle to make their work as disciplinarians reflect their core values; they work to ensure that their actions effectively and fairly serve the students with whom they come in contact. However, along with a concern for fair and appropriate consequences comes the inevitable resistance from teachers, parents, and other administrators: "take no prisoners," "soft on crime," "enabler," and "rescuer" are some of the refrains that new leaders report hearing while they learn to play the role of the enforcer.

Holding students accountable for their behavior can provide authentic opportunities to influence the lives of young people—to get them to be more reflective and to participate more fully in their education. Additionally, the enforcer role sometimes provides school leaders with the occasion to have teachers and parents reflect on the ways in which they work with those individuals who have engaged in negative and disruptive behavior. Of course, it would be foolish to think that new school leaders will not also be shaped by the challenging roles they are expected to play.

SWITCHING ROLES IN MID-PERFORMANCE

One day, Michael C. (September 2002)—a high school assistant principal—approached a student using a cell phone on campus and told him to "put the phone away. Get off. I don't want to see it out. School's out. Move it off campus." Clearly, this is the enforcer speaking. Michael explained that he was just upholding the school policy and did not see his language as provocative. Notice that Michael did not ask the student's name. His sentences were brief, terse, and directive. When the young "Latino boy," as Michael described him, refused to comply, Michael softened his approach: "I asked him again nicely to please put the phone away." Note the adverb "nicely" coupled with the exhortation "please." Again, the student refused to comply, and Michael immediately returned to a more confrontational approach:

> *"You know, what do you want me to do, take the phone?"... And the next thing you know, I had triggered something inside of him and he hung up the phone and he started yelling and screaming and swearing and he wanted to fight me... I didn't touch him, but I kept staying in front of him and said, "You're just going to get into trouble. If you run away and don't tell me your name you're forcing me to take some pretty serious disciplinary action."*

Now we have a real story on our hands, chock-full of emotion and tension. Not only was Michael using the *talk* of the enforcer, he was using the *walk* as well; Michael positioned his body to gain control over the student.

Michael acknowledged that his typical approach to enforcing school policy had been fairly low-key. For example, when he saw kids talking on their cell phones on campus, he generally asked the students to put the phones away. When he used what he described as the "same approach" with this particular student, the results were quite different: "And he started yelling and screaming and swearing and he wanted to fight me, and he threatened that he wanted to throw down." Eventually, the campus police and the dean of students intervened and helped get the student to the office, where they began their proverbial finger wagging and chastising.

During the interrogation, Michael saw the student "shrinking in his chair" and eventually asked the security officer and the dean to leave his office so he could have a real conversation with him:

> *"I know you're looking at me as a white guy in a tie you've never seen before who's telling you your business, and that can't be comfortable." And [the student] cracked this huge smile and started laughing. And we kind of broke it down in the humor level... I was just hoping the kid wouldn't do anything stupid.*

Notice that the issue of race is brought up, although it is never thoroughly explored with the student. Michael is acknowledging the sanctioned and unspoken dynamics of power and control in our schools and in our society. Some of these relationships are positional, whereas others are based on age, race, sexual orientation, and gender. As Michael continued to tell his story, it became clear that he saw himself as an equity promoter. Michael began to consider the political and ethical implications of the actions he was expected to take.

> *Okay, the interesting part of the story was I was caught in a dilemma. Technically, for a student to fight an administrator… that's a recommendation for expulsion… So I have a moral call here… He finally did apologize to me. I talked about the gravity of the situation, and he admitted that he was wrong… And I said, "Well, you know what? I'm not going to suspend you." And I spoke with his mother… and I said what's going to happen is your parents are going to come back here on Monday morning with me, and we're going to have a conference.*

The institution expected an expulsion, but Michael allowed himself to make a "moral call" and defy the system. Michael's story concluded with his discovery that the student had been scheduled for only four classes and was informed of a "proficiency test that he could take in November that would enable him to get out of high school… So it was pretty clear to me that the school had given up on him." Michael mentioned the fact that the student is Latino several times in his narrative; clearly there is the implication of institutional racism. At the conclusion of the narrative, Michael described the process of befriending the student and enrolling him in six classes. So, although he began his narrative describing an emotionally charged situation, he transformed his role from enforcer to equity promoter. Indeed, school leaders have the latitude to choose how they carry out their responsibilities.

ALIGNING SCHOOL POLICY WITH CORE VALUES

In another story that portrays the role of the enforcer, Steven G. (October 2003), a brand new assistant principal in a large elementary school, was charged with "handling" the lion's share of the discipline at his school. He communicated clear vision and values about how students should be disciplined. This became evident as he described his approach to developing a school discipline policy and his compulsion to share his guiding principles with the teachers in his school.

> *It got real ugly, because their whole idea of discipline is really discarding children who they feel are bad kids… This sort of discipline policy would weed out kids and then they would start naming these kids. I got offended, but I understood that they didn't really mean what they said. And I simply stated that… school is a place where you take kids, these tough kids, and you make something out of them. You don't just get rid of them because you want a better day in your world. And they didn't like that answer very much… [I explained] my role is to maintain a fair discipline policy, and this is not a fair discipline policy… whatever you guys want to do I'll support you, but you have to realize that we need to be inclusive and not try to get rid of kids. It's all we're about. And by the grace of God, the secretary called me down.*

Even though Steven believed he was clear and resolute in communicating his philosophy of intervention, he was profoundly relieved when the secretary rescued him from a tense situation. Steven claimed to be a team player—seemingly a promoter of inclusive decision making—but, in the very same sentence, he laid out a bottom line: "whatever you guys want to do I'll support you, but you have to realize that we need to be inclusive and not try to get rid of kids. It's all we're about." This is a very powerful statement and clearly exhibits the power, delicacy, and dichotomy of school leadership. On one hand, the school leader is expected to be a team player and to authentically engage all members of the school community in important decision making. On the other hand, a strong leader expresses clear vision and values. As Steven was walking the tightrope of school leadership, it is no wonder that he was relieved to be "called down" by the secretary; sometimes, even a superhero needs to be rescued.

However, Steven's story did not end there. He indicated in his narrative that there were a lot of conversations taking place throughout the school—some with Steven, and some behind his back. There was a lot of talk about who this leader was and what he stood for. As an enforcer, it is very easy to be misunderstood or misrepresented. Steven chose an instructive approach to clarify his identity as school leader. He wanted the members of his school community to know his guiding principles, to understand where he was coming from, and to understand where he wanted to take the school (at least in the area of discipline). He put his beliefs in writing to make his values and intentions more concrete and tangible:

> *So I published my biography… and I ran off copies of my philosophy of education and I stuck them in everybody's box. To let them know where I am coming from, who I am. Because really, who am I? They have no idea. So I gave them a little bit of background and then, later on that day, I met that guy and I said, "You know, this is where I'm coming from. I don't want to be a stick in the mud. I know we can work this out."*

The distribution of a biography—a vision statement—was not the final product that ensured a neat resolution to his story. Rather, it was a means to an end. Steven was interested in modifying the existing discipline policy. During the reflective storytelling process, the questioners prompted Steven to consider where he was in this change process, and what was happening for him internally as he moved this initiative forward.

Questioner: *I just appreciate that you seemed very uncomfortable to be put in that position. To me, actually, that was really brilliant.*

Steven: **I need as [many] hugs as I can get nowadays.**

Questioner: *What was the reaction to your doing that?*

Steven: **It was mixed. There's approximately 60 teachers in the school, so maybe about 10 of them… it's kind of like the bell curve. You have your 10 who are just like, "Oh, jeez, screw this!" And then you have your guys who say, "Well, maybe… he's doing okay," guys in the middle, and people who are leaning out. And some who are just 100 percent, "Yeah, you need to look at the kids; what the hell's the matter with the rest of the guys?"**

Questioner: *But you took a risk to put yourself out there, I think, more than what you believe...*

Steven: *About 12 people came up and thanked me because it gave background to what I was running. I was never, ever introduced... I pictured myself in my own school having this person come in, and I've been there for a while and I've worked with these guys, and they start coming up with some ideas; I probably would be a little bit tentative myself... If somebody comes back and says, you shouldn't be doing this, [I'll ask]... "Didn't you read what I've written? Haven't you read my philosophy? Don't you know how I feel about these kids? This is where I'm coming from."*

Ultimately, Steven settled on a process in which all members of the teaching staff had a voice in the creation of the new discipline policy. He decided to have the teachers vote on the new discipline policy. Steven did not describe how he settled on this particular process, nor did he explain why or how a two-thirds majority was determined to be the percentage of affirmative votes required for approval. Nonetheless, Steven took bold action to reform the way discipline was carried out in his school community.

HOLDING ADULTS ACCOUNTABLE

In another story, Rhonda C. (October 2003) showed how playing the role of enforcer is not always about adults reprimanding children. Sometimes, this role involves school leaders working to modify the behavior of other adults in the school community. Rhonda, a new assistant principal at a high school with 1,300 students, was in charge of supervising three campus supervisors who were, in turn, responsible for monitoring student behavior.

> *The parents are very, very concerned about safety on the campus... Campus supervisors— even though they don't have the respect of the teachers or administrators—their job is very, very important. Some of the issues that we go over are how to go to a classroom that a teacher has summoned them to, how to approach the teacher, and how to talk with the teacher. But also [how to] escort the student back up to the office. We've had experiences where some campus supervisors have not applied the principles and rules on how to escort students. So I've been an integral, pivotal person in writing letters of reprimand and talking with them, talking with district personnel about their duties and how to go about doing them. So, since coming on board two years ago, [there have been] three campus supervisors I've had to reprimand.*

Rhonda went on to describe her disdain for working with a particular campus supervisor who had been reassigned to her campus. The employee had been reprimanded in the past for sexual harassment and was known to be ineffective in his previous position. Rhonda provided a summary of the background information and her subsequent reaction:

> *The district decides… he's learned his lesson… My principal and other administrators were about to have a fit: "No, we cannot have him because the person that reported [the sexual harassment] is still at our school." The district said, "No, no, he's okay." We have three young campus supervisors, not even thirty years old—two men and a lady. They're about twenty-two and twenty-seven. This particular person is in his early fifties, so right there there's this age gap.*

It is clear from the onset of the story that there is going to be a problem with the returning security officer. Rhonda provided additional information about the systems, policies, and practices that were being developed to ensure the safety of the children. In considering the big picture of campus security, Rhonda felt compelled to intervene—not only with the campus supervisor but also with a group of students who were not held accountable by the campus supervisor in question:

> *While I'm coming down, students start rushing to the area where he is. I don't see him, but I see all the students rushing. I'm telling the students that they need to go to class. Another assistant principal is on that level right where this is starting to happen… He sees that the campus supervisor is frozen. He sees the student start the fight before he gets there, and he sees the campus supervisor no more than ten feet away from this student that starts to fight. He doesn't see the campus supervisor doing anything. In the meantime, the other campus supervisors rush to the area. They break up the fight—the other two younger ones. He's still standing with a drainage grate that he's picked up in his hand. He has it in his hand, frozen, standing there… And students there see his behavior. And they see that he did not intervene and he did not try to stop them verbally or with his hands pull them apart.*

Notice that the word *frozen* is used two times and that three statements describe what this supervisor is "not" doing. This situation can be seen as an extended metaphor that depicts an organization suffering from paralysis. These systemic problems—when not addressed early—can develop into much larger issues, creating feelings of hopelessness and giving students tacit approval to ignore school rules. The drainage grate, and the fact that it remains in the hand of a campus supervisor during a very heated and potentially dangerous situation, becomes a powerful symbol of a dysfunctional, ineffective individual clutching the wrong tool for the situation.

When Rhonda investigated the impetus of the violent situation, she elucidated her perceptions in no uncertain terms: "It turns into a black and white racial thing. Students go home and tell their parents that this campus supervisor wasn't doing anything. They're coming down on us saying, 'What is going on with this campus?'" Rhonda recognized that the problem was much bigger than a personnel issue with a campus supervisor. Nonetheless, she chose to focus her initial efforts on working directly with the campus supervisor. Rhonda understood that this particular employee was a huge liability:

> *I had to give him a letter of reprimand. He's very upset. My administrator is telling me that I've got to give him this letter… He was out in the parking lot. I told him I needed to talk to him. I tried at*

lunch to give him the letter. He said he didn't want the letter. He said he wanted his union rep there. I said that was fine. He said that he didn't want to get his union rep and that I should get him. I talked to the other administrator, who said, "No way do you talk to his union rep. You don't do anything! You just invite him to your office and give him the letter." I invited him to the office later in the day, with another [assistant principal] there, and I gave him the letter. He protested. He was angry and upset.

Rhonda was still trying to figure out her role and corresponding responsibilities when the custodian told Rhonda that she should arrange a meeting with the union representative. Wisely, she solicited input from her colleague to learn the proper protocol for issuing a letter of reprimand. It is not surprising that the letter became a real object of power in this story. Putting things in writing can elicit strong emotion; it can also prompt an individual—and even an institution—to change.

The conclusion of Rhonda's story allowed her to consider how she could have handled the situation differently. She wasn't sure about her responsibility to contact the union representative, and she allowed the confrontation to occur in a public venue: "Instead of standing there listening, I should have said, 'We need to have this conversation in my office.'" Rhonda knew her intended outcome: she was very committed to ensuring safety on the school campus, and she knew she needed to establish systems and practices that would be followed by all members of the school community. However, she was having difficulty figuring out all of the details and protocols necessary to play the role of enforcer effectively.

Being an enforcer is all about rule making and enforcing. At the end of the day, if rules were clear and everyone followed them, it would be unnecessary for anyone to play the role of enforcer. If leadership were all about enforcing rules and adhering to policy, schools would simply hire policemen instead of principals or assistant principals. Unfortunately, rules and expectations often are not clear, understood, or embraced by all members of the school community. Some students, teachers, support staff, and other administrators believe that the rules are not fair or that they do not apply to them. Many believe that they will not get caught if they break a rule or that there won't be significant consequences if they do. Because our schools are filled with human beings, there will always be individuals who play the role of rule breaker. Therefore, school leaders will be expected to play the role of enforcer and uphold the rules, norms, and expectations of the school community.

School leaders, like many other adults, often become frustrated when students (and other adults) fail to adhere to the rules and expectations of the community. Although many individuals have the luxury of simply ignoring inappropriate behavior, the school leader needs to ensure that the school environment is safe, orderly, and conducive to learning. Maslow (1943) reminds us that physical and emotional safety are two of the most basic human needs. Students are not likely to learn and thrive unless the adults who have been granted the privilege of working with them have fostered a school culture and climate that is safe and nurturing for all members of the school community.

Disturbingly, the aggregate of leadership narratives shows how easily school leaders can be drawn into the archetypal power struggle. Many school leaders wholeheartedly embody the *voice* and *body* of authority, which may not necessarily create optimal conditions for growth and development in our young people or adults. A prime takeaway here is this: good leadership is not just about the rules. More often than not, it's about how they are enforced. Just as a fierce and oppressive parent can contribute to the development of a defiant or disengaged child, so too can school leaders affect the behavior and learning of the students they serve.

Again, it is not uncommon for new leaders to experience internal struggles as they seek to understand their new responsibilities and inhabit their new roles. As school leaders learn to play this critical role, they rarely have time to reflect on the ways in which their thoughts, words, and actions influence the lives of the individuals with whom they work. Even though new leaders may struggle with the challenges of disciplining students in our schools and playing the role of the enforcer, it is important to remember that concerns about the behavior and values of our young people have been around for quite some time:

> *Our youth now love luxury. They have bad manners, contempt for authority; they show disrespect for their elders and love chatter in places of exercise. They no longer rise when elders enter the room. They contradict their parents, chatter before company, gobble food and tyrannize their teachers. (Socrates, fifth century B.C.)*

Engaging in a process of reflective storytelling can extract school leaders from their prescribed roles and allow them the opportunity to review not only their objectives but the means by which they are striving to reach them. This, then, is where school leaders have tremendous autonomy: in their tone and tenor, in their language and the way they position their body, in their interpretation of the rules and expected consequences, and in their beliefs about the motivation and character of the individuals with whom they work. School leaders can benefit from sharing stories with colleagues who are willing to focus a bright spotlight on their thoughts, words, and actions when playing the role of enforcer.

Reflective Questions for Prospective and Practicing School Leaders

- Recall a time in your life when you got in trouble for doing something wrong. How were you treated? What was most painful for you? What did you learn?

- How does the parent community expect you to play the role of enforcer in your school? How is this different from the expectations of teachers or higher-level administrators?

- How might the role of enforcer be played differently?

- What underlying message are you conveying to students (or teachers or parents) when you let them know that they have violated a rule or exhibited inappropriate behavior?

- What is your body language communicating when you hold others accountable? What tone of voice are you using? What are some of the common refrains in the vocabulary that you use?

- What role do race, gender, and social class play when we discipline students?

- How would you respond if you noticed that you were suspending a disproportionate number of students of color? Whom might you engage to address this situation?

- Is there another language that administrators could be trained to use when disciplining students? Are there certain words, phrases, and voice tones that you should avoid when playing the role of enforcer?

- Is there a situation in which you would ignore inappropriate or illegal behavior?

- How do you discipline and socialize students without quashing their individuality?

- What can be done so that students and teachers learn to hold each other accountable rather than the sole responsibility falling on the shoulders of the school leader?

The School Leader as System Builder

I found that at my school you have to start small and build. I almost feel like I have to sneak it in, go backdoor…

Gretchen S., December 2003

Surprisingly, *system builder* was a role described with great frequency in the narratives shared by new administrators in our study. This was unexpected, because challenging the status quo involves a certain amount of risk; it has the potential to elicit anger and frustration in some of the stakeholder groups who may not be interested in enduring any kind of change process. Of the 246 narratives we reviewed, 57 (23 percent) described explicit system challenging or system building as a primary role. Of course, challenging a system will overlap and intersect with many of the other roles and responsibilities school leaders are expected to play.

Being a system builder is an outgrowth of serving as an operations manager. As much as school leaders would like to focus on instructional leadership, they are equally responsible for the maintenance of facilities, budgets, personnel requirements, and state- and federal-compliance mandates. Each of these job expectations can pull the school leader away from his or her instructional priorities. Yet, resourceful school leaders are expected to find ways to do all of their work more efficiently and effectively. They will take the time after engaging in a particular initiative to consider what went well and what went wrong. They will continually engage in a process of systems thinking—in which they consider the lessons learned from an organizational perspective—and they will make the necessary changes and work with others in the school community to foster a culture of continuous improvement. Marzano (2003) argues that achievement-oriented leaders will allocate some of their time to ensure that the school runs efficiently, which may, in turn, have a more positive impact on student learning than reviewing lesson plans or addressing instructional challenges.

Whereas many of the roles and activities of the school leader are clearly defined and communicated by the upper-level administrators in the organization, the role of system builder is unique in that it generally falls outside of the prescribed job expectations: "change agent" typically is not listed in school leader job descriptions. Being a system builder requires going above and beyond the demands of the various stakeholder groups connected to the school community. But what prompts a new administrator to make decisions and take actions, to challenge a component of the existing system or build a new system?

37

The role of system builder requires a specialized set of skills and strategies that begin with a process of needs identification. In any given school, there is a litany of problems worthy of attention. Problem recognition, problem framing, and the act of prioritizing a particular problem require big-picture thinking and valuing. Taking on almost any challenge presents an element of political risk as well as the possibility for conflict and strong emotion. Deutschman (2005) explores how resistant most people are to change, even when refusing to change could result in a premature death. In studying a group of individuals who underwent coronary-bypass grafting, he reports that two years after their surgeries 90 percent of the individuals had not changed their related lifestyle behaviors (smoking, eating, drinking, and stress-inducing activities). If a "well-informed, trusted authority figure [like a doctor cannot prompt] enduring changes in the way [individuals] think and act," it is easy to understand why school leaders face Sisyphus-like challenges in motivating members of a school community to make changes in their professional practice.

But what systems and structures should be challenged or built within the world of education? How might the construction of a particular system ensure greater consistency, coherence, and clarity in the practice of the school leader? A review of leadership narratives indicates that new administrators undertake three primary areas when playing the role of system builder: systems and structures, attitudes and beliefs, and collaboration.

SYSTEMS AND STRUCTURES

It seems perverse to say that problems are our friends, but we cannot develop effective responses to complex situations unless we actively seek and confront the real problems which are in fact difficult to solve. Problems are our friends because it is only through immersing ourselves in problems that we can come up with creative solutions.

—Michael Fullan, 1993

The phrase *systems and structures* refers to the specific policies and practices that are codified (and thereby provide clear direction) and make the expectations of educators who are operating in the organization more explicit. The school leader, in an attempt to make sense of the work and in a desire to get things done more efficiently, often bumps up against the fact that there is no rhyme or reason to how different areas of the school are organized and structured. This can include anything from lunch schedules to discipline policies to intervention programs. Thus, the desire to impose order, to clarify roles and responsibilities, and to establish processes that can be used to make decisions often are primary areas of focus for new administrators.

ATTITUDES AND BELIEFS

The key here is not the kind of instruction but the attitude underlying it. When teachers do not understand the potential of the students they teach, they will underteach them no matter what the methodology.

—Lisa Delpit, 1995

New administrators struggle with ways to influence or modify the beliefs, attitudes, assumptions, and expectations of individuals and groups within the school setting. This struggle, when depicted in leadership narratives, often focuses on beliefs about student learning and who is able to learn. New administrators challenge racial, socioeconomic, and gender-based biases with outrage and zeal. Whereas low expectations can characterize the practice of an ineffective educator, system builders work to implement new systems, practices, and protocols that might facilitate (or require) members of the school community to methodically explore and modify debilitating attitudes and beliefs. This idea will be explored in greater detail when we examine the role of equity promoter.

COLLABORATION

We can build "learning organizations," organizations where people continually expand their capacity to create the results they truly desire, where new and expansive patterns of thinking are nurtured, where collective aspiration is set free, and where people are continually learning how to learn together.

—Peter Senge, 1990

Whereas "belief systems" might answer the question "What is to be the area of focus?" and "systems and structures" describes the framework within which the work will get done, "collaboration" answers the questions "Who will determine the work that gets done?" and "Who is expected to get the work done?" Many new administrators describe scenarios in which they are actively working to create collaborative structures and dismantle the top-down hierarchy that typifies traditional, factory-model organizations. When teachers and support staff are authentically involved in curricular and policy changes, they are more likely to implement the changes and take ownership in making them work (Sprague 1973). It is important to note that an emphasis on collaboration and shared decision making is now an integral part of the training in many administrative preparation programs.

Being a system builder is much easier said than done. Great tension often exists when one is working within the system and trying to reform it at the same time. Issues of maintaining one's personal integrity rub up against systems and structures that may have been in place for decades. An underlying feeling of job insecurity often emerges in stories about challenging a system. The question of how hard to push is discussed frequently among new leaders, who often raise the question "Is this an issue I am willing to lose my job over?"

CALCULATING HOW HARD TO PUSH

Henry K. (September 2002), a middle school assistant principal, signaled a desire to engage in system building as he began his story with a parable that depicted a common theme discussed by many new school leaders: bold leadership. Subthemes of race and equity—which are profoundly significant in urban schools—were gently woven into Henry's story, foreshadowing the issues to be explored:

> *And if you know [this district office administrator], she's a very strong-willed, small black woman who just can kind of take on a room. But she said something very interesting: the day she learned how to become a school administrator was the day she didn't care if she was fired. When I first came to [my school], I came on the heels of the former administrator… this person was a hurricane… And I said, well, you don't have to worry about me, I'm more of a tropical depression.*

Henry used self-deprecating humor in describing himself as a "tropical depression," but he then described his challenge of trying to hire a special education teacher who had been given a bad recommendation in the district. Hiring the "best and the brightest" and "recruit and retain" are just two of the common refrains in the world of education. In the beginning of Henry's story, he was filled with hope about the possibility of filling a very difficult position, that of a special education teacher.

> *So I get this call from this young man. And he says he's in the special ed. program and is very interested in coming out and touring the school and interviewing for the job. And I said great, come out. He comes out and he's this rather kind of mod young African American male… we ended up talking for two hours. You know, I asked the typical questions of how much time do you have in the credential program, what's your experience, have you ever filled out an IEP [individualized education plan], this kind of thing. But then we ended up having this really wonderful, deep conversation about teaching and learning; and it doesn't really matter what population you teach, all kids need quality teachers. So I was left with this really wonderful feeling about this guy.*

Henry was excited to have found an African American man who had a degree in special education, one of the teaching areas with the most severe shortages. Very soon, however, Henry learned that this particular teacher had been "released" by another principal in the district, which meant that he was ineligible for rehire.

A conflict within a story often takes the form of a direct challenge: a villain appears, or the hero must address the lack of a basic need (Propp 1958). The hero in this story, Henry, is compelled to fight to get this teacher on his team. This is not an easy role for a new administrator to play. Internally, it was very challenging for Henry; he did quite a bit of soul-searching during the initial phase of his decision-making process.

> *I said, okay, I just can't let this go. I cannot let this go. So I immediately e-mailed [the principal] saying, "Look, this is our population. These kids have been denied so much in their lives. The only thing they have right now is this school. So, what can we do to turn this school around, make it so that it's the one thing they look forward to during the day? They don't have their clothes. They don't have anything. So what can we do?" She doesn't e-mail me back, so the next morning I call her; I say, "I have to talk to you. Drop what you're doing."... I explain the situation, "Ninety percent of the kids are African American, we have to start balancing the faculty out and bring in some people that can relate to these kids." So she goes, "Okay, okay, I hear you. Tell you what I'm going to do. I'm going to go down to Human Resources, I'm going to get this other woman placed, and then we'll see about getting this guy."*

This is how we do battle in education. We do not dramatically unsheathe actual swords. Rather, we e-mail people. We raise our voices emphatically—often in the solitude of our offices, occasionally in faculty meetings or public venues. But Henry's hopefulness was quickly dashed. He received a clue that he might not achieve his intended results when his principal failed to return phone calls or e-mails. Finally, the conversation with the principal led to an unfortunate climax of the story:

> *"Did you talk about this gentleman?" "Yes I did. You can't hire him." And I said, "Why?" She said, "Because he's known. He's been marked. He's been blacklisted." "Oh my God. I've just spent two hours in conversation with this kid, he's come to the school, he's shown a real, deep appreciation for what he does, and we're going to blow him off because some principal at another school was so powerful that she can get rid of anybody. This is where we're at?" And [she] said, "This is where we're at." And I said, "Great."*

Unfortunately, in educational administration, stories do not always have happy endings. Sometimes large, urban school districts present barriers that even the bold, principle-driven superhero cannot leap over or walk around. Many of the stories captured in the reflective storytelling process do not have endings at all. The fact that the reader and the researcher alike may never learn how the situation turns out can be very frustrating indeed.

It is heartening to note that new administrators are using the reflective storytelling process to better frame the challenges at hand and figure out next steps. In Henry's story, he began to engage in a process of consequence analysis, with the support, guidance, and questioning of his colleagues. Henry examined his guiding principles and his internal limits as he began to wrestle with the stark realization that there were no satisfactory options:

> *I thought to myself, the previous administrator would have hung up the phone, called this kid and hired him, and just taken the consequences. And I just said, "Am I strong enough to do that right now?" I've been here four weeks—how do I push for this? How do you override not just one principal, but another very powerful principal in the district, and the district office, to get someone in who might be able to do some good at this school? So that's kind of where I was left at three o'clock this afternoon. What to do now? Um, that's kind of what I'm struggling with here. You know, part of me says, well… what do I have to lose? Just put me back in the classroom.*

This is not merely a story about being a system builder; this is a story about a new administrator searching for identity in, and ownership of, a new position. Clearly, Henry was also playing the role of equity promoter. He was eager to support the hiring of an African American male to work with a primarily African American population. But was he so committed to his guiding principles that he was willing to lose his job over it? Does giving up on a particular issue, person, or mission mean that a school leader has no personal integrity? These are the kinds of questions that administrators must confront on a regular basis. This is what it means to be a system builder.

SCORCHING BRIDGES FOR A CLEAN SCHOOL

In another story of system building, Debbie M. (October 2003)—a second-year elementary school assistant principal—was working with her principal to identify an area of responsibility that would enable her to develop a new set of leadership skills. Debbie was able to recognize a problem in her school, but, as we will soon learn, she failed to effectively communicate the issue to key stakeholders in her decision-making/action-taking process:

> *[The principal] asked me, "What do you want to do?… What do you want to work on?" So we negotiated that, and one of the things that I took on was sort of a quasi-supervisor role for our facilities department, that being the head custodian and the night crew… I knew that was an area overall in which I absolutely did not have any expertise… One of our regular [custodians] went out on long-term disability, so we're down to our two guys and then a substitute custodian. And then one of the other guys had a car accident and he was out. The bottom line is we haven't been getting support. Sometimes we have our day guy and maybe somebody who comes for four hours to clean up.*

The custodians charged with cleaning the school were not on-site, which meant that they were not able to keep the school clean. Debbie was clear about the challenge she was facing, and she had conversations with her principal about possible approaches to take. Next, Debbie shared some of her knowledge of district-level protocols that she believed would help her address the site issues:

> *By contract the teachers have this procedure, [this form] they turn in... whenever they feel like it, and it says the things that weren't done. So those things get turned in to me because I'm in charge of facilities. And I collect them... and I fax them to the assistant superintendent. I was doing that on a real regular basis... The fast response team would come out and say, "What do you mean the garbage isn't emptied? What do you mean the floors haven't been swept?" So they're not exactly happy.*

The dilemma, of course, is that these forms were not designed to address problems such as a shortage of staff. They were intended to monitor the performance of custodians who are actually on the job. Debbie recognized that the tool she had been using would not address the situation, so she decided to write a comprehensive memo to the assistant superintendent and to the head of maintenance and operations. First, the fast response team was unhappy, and then the assistant superintendent was really unhappy:

> *He's calling me on the phone screaming at me, literally, "Why are you sending all these in? I don't see you writing up these custodians!" So I said, "Are you telling me you don't wanna see these forms? Are you telling me not to follow the contract?" And I said, "I can't write up a custodian who's not here! What can I do?"*

When building new systems, there are no simple answers. Site leaders often must contend with strong emotions to get things done. Initially, in this story, it did not seem like it would be a profound challenge to clear up the current misunderstanding; however, Debbie remained a target of intense emotion:

> *So the superintendent calls and she is screaming at me! "Why are we getting all these forms? Why aren't you writing these people up?" And then I started to say something and she stopped and said, "You're not listening to me." And she goes right on screaming. My principal is sitting there and I'm sitting there with the phone, going GRRRRR! because I stopped talking. I knew she just needed to rage. And I just let her rage on and on and on. It was really bad. The implication was "You've got a few squeaky wheels [teachers] here; why aren't you taking care of them?" I said, "That's one strategy. I'll take that into consideration." By the end of the conversation she stopped yelling long enough to hear me say that I can't write the custodian up if he isn't here.*

Unfortunately, simple but important issues like maintaining a clean learning environment can require tremendous efforts, especially when the bureaucracy of a large school district is involved. Debbie did not give up, but clearly her frustration was mounting. In her narrative, Debbie was especially reflective and able to maintain her big-picture thinking.

> *I don't think it's a good thing to have the superintendent either yell at you or know your name that well. I debriefed with my principal, and I sat down and I said, "You know, this is… just driving me crazy. I've got these wonderful people that are helping me at this school, this wonderful profession, and I go in in the morning and I say, 'I'm not going to do this facility [related work] today, I am going to do teaching and learning today.' And two hours later I'm like, GRRRR!"*

But changes were taking place. They may not have been systemic changes, but the facility would be cleaner as a result of Debbie's actions:

> *One thing that has happened is we have made such a huge, huge deal out of this that we are getting a sub custodian. And we're getting one of the best people. That's really good, but I know in the process some bridges have been, if not burned, scorched. And I don't know whether that's going to come back to bite me. I don't think I did anything wrong. I wish I had been able to intervene between… I did a good job of intervening between the teachers and the issue so they felt like I was doing right by them.*

Debbie did a fine job supporting the teachers in her school and addressing, at least in the short term, the problem she had identified. The institution, as a whole, became aware of the custodial problem at Debbie's site. But was this worth the cost of burning and scorching bridges? Is there something Debbie could have done differently? Could she have worked more closely with district office personnel to address the shortage of custodians at her site? Would she have made the same decisions if she had known how many people she would anger in the process? These are the questions of a reflective practitioner, of a school leader interested in getting things done.

GUIDING TEAMS PAST ADMINISTRATIVE ROADBLOCKS

Iris P. (September 2002), a brand new elementary assistant principal serving as a system builder, began her narrative by downplaying the significance of her story. She spoke in broken sentences and qualifiers that signaled some tentativeness in finding her way as a new school leader. The way she settled on this story seemed to parallel the way she settled on the development of a 9/11 memorial assembly at her school. The idea appeared to occur by happenstance:

> *I don't have any profound stories that… not really, I kind of expected… [the principal] is kind of protecting me from the real dirt that's going on in the school. And I don't get played off of him by the teachers, so I'm trying to take my thing… and not get involved in some of the stuff that's going on. So I… wanted to do a 9/11 assembly and… [the principal] says, "Why?"*

Iris talked about her intention to "not get involved in some of the stuff that's going on." By this, she may mean a desire to avoid the political and emotionally charged issues with which her principal was grappling. Although the creation of a 9/11 assembly may seem to be a small, contained project, many new school leaders don't recognize the efforts required to get some of these initiatives off the ground. When they settle on an idea, they don't always consider the magnitude of the roadblocks they might encounter. When the principal asked the provocative question "Why?" he did not wait for a response from Iris. According to Iris, he launched into a series of statements and questions intended to discourage Iris's initiative:

> "The kids really don't do anything like that. It's not really necessary to do anything like that... you probably won't be able to do that this year. The teachers always do their own thing... Why don't you do this? Why don't you have a meeting at a time when the teachers show up [if] they want to?"

Through her persistence, Iris was able to get her principal to agree on the project, albeit unenthusiastically. Without checking with Iris, he wrote an informational memo to teachers that Iris described as "cryptic, and I wasn't sure if I read it, I would understand what it was all about." Iris did not think the principal's note would do the trick of garnering teacher buy-in, so she chose to take matters into her own hands:

> So I... went around and rattled people on my own, and a lot of teachers showed up, and I ended up having every grade level participate. The fourth and fifth grade had a poem they wrote, the third graders sang "Lean on Me"... the second graders did the peace pledge, and the kindergartners and first graders decorated... And it was... a nice thing because the school doesn't do a lot of things together...

At this point in the story, one of the reflective questioners probed Iris, seeking more information about the relational dynamics with the principal. There seemed to be some tension in the situation. Although Iris claimed that the principal was often misunderstood, she also did not want him to derail her initiative.

> I felt like he would have proved himself right and proved me wrong if no one came to the meeting... And I would have felt more than wrong, I would have felt like he doesn't feel the need for this whole school collaboration and leadership... he feels like being really top-down.

So, although this could be thought of as a minor, isolated project, Iris believed that the initiative served as a model for the principal and the teachers about how to work together collaboratively. Iris believed that, if she could change the way business was conducted in her school, this would show teachers and staff how they might engage differently (and more collaboratively), which could lead to transformations in the school culture. This approach is a clear model for system building.

Although the reflective storytelling process is primarily designed to promote reflection, there is room for reinforcement and celebration. One listener said, "You didn't just sit back and let that happen… you went the extra step to make it happen. And it was successful."

The beauty of system building is that once new systems have been set in place and all of the stakeholder groups understand the corresponding expectations, there may be less need for the school leader to play the role of enforcer. The system builder is the polar extreme of the stereotypical bureaucrat who pushes paper, keeps the system running smoothly, and effectively maintains the status quo. Those leaders who are willing to stand up and work to make positive changes in an entrenched bureaucracy give hope and inspiration to all members of the school community:

Each time a person stands up for an ideal, or acts to improve the lot of others, or strikes out against injustice, he/she sends forth a tiny ripple of hope… and crossing each other from a million different centers of energy and daring, those ripples build a current that can sweep down the mightiest walls of oppression and resistance. (Kennedy 1966)

It is understandable that school leaders would not tell stories in which they present themselves as managers who are content to allow the school to continue down its present path while maintaining the mantra "Business has always been done this way." Nonetheless, the specificity in the stories illustrates the fact that school leaders are, in fact, risk takers, action takers, movers and shakers—the kinds of individuals who deal directly with issues and makes things happen for others. But playing the role of system builder is not necessarily about seeking attention or accolades. In fact, effective system builders can be invisible to teachers because they readily provide resources and establish structures without being asked; this allows teachers to focus their attention on student learning rather than the operations of the school. Indeed, a smooth-running, efficient school organization can help to provide students, teachers, and support staff with feelings of safety and security, which—according to Maslow (1943)—are basic human needs.

Although new school leaders often are eager to take up arms to fix a system or structure, in analyzing their narratives it becomes clear that many leaders simply get ready, fire, and aim! In other words, they don't seem to think out the problem-solving strategy and all of the corresponding implications before they plunge headfirst into troubled waters. They rarely take the necessary time to engage in a root cause analysis or to measure how deeply the problem is embedded within the school culture. Sometimes, in their haste to fix a problem, they fail to engage key stakeholders in the decision-making process, thus frustrating and alienating many caring individuals in the school community. There is an old African proverb that reminds us, "If you want to go fast, go alone. If you want to go far, go together."

Engaging in a process of reflective storytelling within a professional learning community can provide valuable opportunities for school leaders to consider the ramifications and implications of solving a problem. Colleagues who are willing to ask challenging questions that might spawn reflection and interrupt an ill-fated course of action are essential as well. Problem framing, values clarification, stakeholder involvement, and increasing the clarity of desired outcomes are essential ingredients to effective problem-solving and can be explored collectively in a structured storytelling process (this will be described in greater detail in Chapter 7).

Over time, many school leaders learn the importance of developing authentic professional learning communities on their school campuses, thus increasing the level of buy-in toward the change processes that are under way and fostering a greater sense of commitment and connectedness among participants. Not only does authentic collaboration meet a basic human need of belongingness (Maslow 1943), it also can help members of the school community feel connected and part of something larger than themselves. This, in turn, can have the added benefit of increasing teacher retention.

Collaboration with one's colleagues seems likely to generate not only shared goals but also goals which have highly motivating properties. Collaboration requires one to put one's purposes in words and to be clear enough to explain one's purposes to others. Furthermore, the public nature of such interaction creates pressure to set goals which seem worthwhile to others and therefore are not likely to be trivial. (Leithwood and Steinbach 1995, 100)

Reflective Questions for Prospective and Practicing School Leaders

- What are some of the inefficiencies or irritants in your school community that you believe require fixing? How urgent are these challenges?

- Do you have enough information to fully understand the nature and root causes of these challenges?

- What are the underlying values associated with these challenges that you have identified?

- What is the best approach to bring up these challenges?

- As a school leader, do you generally offer suggestions or recommendations, or do you set expectations?

- What is the worst possible outcome if you choose to take on these challenges?

- What are some of the structures in your school that take away from the focus on teaching and learning?

- Do members of your school community generally support you in your initiatives? Why or why not?

- Are there currently structures in place that allow members of your school community to raise issues and concerns about systems in your school that they would like addressed or modified?

- What happens to individuals in your school who "speak their truth" when their truth bumps up against community norms?

- What are some of the ways that you have solicited support or involvement to make changes in your school?

- Who are some of the individuals who present as a political threat in making change? What are some of the most effective ways to work with these individuals?

- Are some issues or challenges in your school simply too hot to handle? Why is this so?

- Are there any systemic problems in your school community that you simply cannot live with—that you would be willing to lose your job for if the issues could not be resolved?

- If you are willing to compromise on a particular issue, does this mean that you do not have integrity as a school leader?

Chapter 4

THE SCHOOL LEADER AS EQUITY PROMOTER

They're probably going to hear me on the phone and know that I'm white and they're going to make impressions and decisions about who it is that I am, and why it is that I'm telling them I'm suspending your kid or why it is that I'm disciplining one of their kids. And it's different with parents because you only get this one time… and they don't see everything about you. When you're in the classroom and you have minority kids, they still see the white teacher, they still see the white face and then see you disciplining them, and they also see you doing lots of things to show that you love and care for them. But the parents come in and they see this snapshot.

Max L., October 2003

In their stories, school leaders regularly describe their personal challenges and fears in addressing emotionally charged and important issues that involve issues of race and equity; however, it is inspiring to hear how they continue to play the role of *equity promoter* with such passion and courage. Issues of equity can be found when looking at data on student achievement, discipline, teacher hiring practices, allocation of resources, and the engagement of different parent communities. When William S. (November 2002) was setting up an after-school program for underachieving students (all of whom happened to be African American), he was accused of attempting to "resegregate the school." As he shared this story with his colleagues, he shook his head and said, "Let no good deed go unpunished!" He then went on to talk about what he described as his moral obligation to ensure that all of the students in his school were learning: "I can't stand aside and let our children fail!" Ellinor and Gerard provide ample warning about the ways in which our fears can lead to paralysis:

It is fear that makes talking about diversity so difficult. Fear that I will say something that will offend you or reveal my ignorance or prejudices. Fear that you will think less of me after I speak… We need to be and feel heard, to be willing to listen without feeling that we must change to conform to another's way of thinking and being. Until we can create a place for such conversations to occur, I doubt we will be able to create new ways of being together that honor us all. (1998, 276)

Although equity promoter was the primary role described in 32 (14 percent) of the 246 narratives, issues of equity and justice were peppered throughout the vast majority of them. For narratives to be coded as equity promoter stories, school leaders needed to describe efforts to confront issues of racism, sexism, homophobia, and discrimination based on religion, language, socioeconomics, or age. Approximately half of the equity promoter stories involved school leaders playing the role of child advocate. One could make the case that the discrimination students experience based on their age or their position at the bottom of the organizational hierarchy should not be compared to other forms of discrimination or prejudice. However, it is my contention that individuals who experience pain or challenge as a direct or indirect result of power imbalances are worthy of acknowledgment, dialogue, and deliberate action to address the inequity.

There are problems with lumping all of the equity-related issues together in a short chapter on leadership roles and development. While nearly every challenge that educators face contains substantive issues related to equity, it is important to note that each inequity perpetuated by our schools and districts has a different flavor and feel. DeCuir and Dixson explain:

> *Race, and experiences based on race, are not equal. Thus the experiences that people of color have with respect to race and racism create an unequal situation.* Equity, *however, recognizes that the playing field is unequal and attempts to address the inequality. (2004, 29)*

School leaders tell equity stories for many reasons. First of all, powerful emphasis is placed on issues of equity, justice, and social responsibility in many administrative preparation programs. Second, the choice to work in an urban school environment tends to attract those school leaders who have a passion for addressing head-on the equity issues so pervasive in our schools and our society. Indeed, addressing issues of equity in our public school system and closing the achievement gap are arguably the most important challenges that school leaders will confront. In his book *Courageous Conversations,* Glen Singleton asks, "To what degree do you and your system have the will, skill, knowledge and capacity to understand and address issues of race as they relate to existing racial achievement disparities?" (Singleton and Linton 2006, 2).

One of the many challenges is that—regardless of our intentions and desire to create an equitable learning environment—all members of the school community bring with them their own experiences and backgrounds, their own biases:

> *Teacher [and principal] perceptions of students are grounded in their own location in social categories of race, class, and gender. They make sense of their interactions with pupils and the conditions of their work from these social locations. Teachers bring different experiences and knowledge of racial structures into schools that provide a framework from which to interpret, to organize information, to act. (Ferguson 2000, 89)*

From reading the 246 narratives, one might think that a school leader—the unassuming superhero—flies from one injustice to another, preventing one suspension based on race from taking place here and ensuring equal access to curriculum there. Remember Henry K., the system builder, who was passionate about hiring an African American teacher who had been blacklisted by the district. Remember Michael C., who transformed his enforcer role to that of equity promoter by challenging a student about his use of a cell phone on campus and eventually changing the student's schedule to ensure that the student would meet graduation requirements. In each of these instances, school leaders were struggling to address inequities that they identified in the field.

One unique feature of administrative storytelling is the fact that many of the narratives begin with an abstract that reviews the ethnic composition of the school. It is a quick and efficient way to make other administrators aware of some of the implicit equity-related challenges that the school leader may be facing:

> [The] high school [has] approximately 1,430 students. Largest ethnic group is Chinese, Asian American; second largest group is European American; and the next largest group is Latino. Seventy-nine percent of the Asian American students meet the Cal State UC requirements… and achievement. European American: 42 percent meet the Cal State University requirements; and our Latino population: approximately 14 percent meet the Cal State University requirements. So the achievement gap is definitely prevalent, and that's what we're working on. (James S., October 2003)

For school leaders, such a demographic overview is a way to signal to other educators that they are knowledgeable about their school site and that they understand that equity issues are part of the work. Words and phrases like *achievement gap, disadvantaged, disenfranchised,* and *marginalized* appear throughout many of the narratives that new school leaders share.

DAMAGING BEAUTIFICATION

Anne T. (October 2002), a new assistant principal in a high school, presented a poignant narrative in which she was caught off guard and thrust into the role of equity promoter. Anne began her story by expressing an earnest desire to help with a campus beautification project, part of the development of a new identity for her school.

> My school took over a new… school site… from a school that had been in existence for thirty years and so there was all its culture… And the move itself… caused a little bit of unrest with the minority community. And so one of the things that happened late in the summer, early in the school year, was this need for the students and for the parents… to somehow make this campus their own… there's a big sign that [has the name of the old school]. And it was supposed to be changed, at first it was supposed to be taken off altogether… and nothing has happened yet.

This sounds like a relatively simple challenge for the new assistant principal: to serve as a community builder. But in the first passage of her narrative, Anne provided hints that her story would ultimately be about equity; she foreshadowed to the listener that "the move itself… caused a little bit of unrest with the minority community." Anne further positioned herself as a leader who understood the need for students and parents "to somehow make this campus their own." The underlying values being expressed here—her guiding principles—include *respect* and *inclusion*. Because these basic values were not being expressed in her school community, Anne decided that she was going to take some kind of action and make a difference.

> *So we put together a beautification team… we brought in an artist from the community; he's a volunteer. And he created this plan, this master plan for the quad courtyard area to make it kind of… it's a predominantly white school, and this is important because [the former school] was predominantly not white. And his vision was to make it have kind of this one… city streetscape kind of feel… the assistant principal, who is in charge of facilities, did not think it was a good idea, but we went with it.*

Notice how the issues of equity are continually raised. This is not merely hinting of the trouble yet to come. Clearly, this is an area of passion and concern for Anne:

> *[The principal and I] had asked on more than one occasion, is there anything here… is there anything here that's protected? The outgoing principal said, "I'm not really sure, I don't know." There was a mural that was painted through part of a… federal grant in homage to Cesar Chavez that our community painted over in one fell swoop with a giant red block of paint. That's all it is. Not with another mural, just kind of splat! As one of the students said, "With the splash of a brush, you wiped us out."*

In Anne's story, the red paint served as the catalyst for profound unrest and reflection. Very often, images and objects can be seen as captivating metaphors that depict underlying struggles. As the student complained, "We weren't allowed to even wear red on this campus because of what it signifies in the city. And in my country, in my culture, red is the color of battle. You've gone to war with us symbolically." Although the beautification committee began with a noble intention—to bring the community together—they effectively disenfranchised an entire ethnic group. How could something like this happen? Anne struggled to make sense of a horrific situation:

> *There was a big ceremony that the outgoing teachers attended… you know, we had some culpability in terms of not recognizing that this was something… we should have been, like, "not that one over there." Anyway, we have a predominantly white committee that's sitting in this room and being asked, "Why did you do this?" by the muralist. It was a federal grant, so they came out to videotape it to prove to the government and the grantor that this actually happened. And it was going to be part of the Mural March.*

Anne used the word *culpability* to describe her feelings of responsibility for the travesty. This mistake—this insensitivity—was being broadcast beyond the boundaries of the beautification committee as well.

There were videotapes, federal monies, and a very public mural march. How does a new administrator who is interested in serving as an equity promoter possibly fix something like this? How could she find a way to rectify this situation? How uncomfortable must it be for a new school leader to engage in a process of reflection, to look in the mirror and recognize that she was the authority figure? As the equity promoter, Anne understood that she was the person responsible for righting the wrong:

> *It was awful. And so the muralist, the woman who was working with the university, [began working with] the students, a body of these students who… they just make you weep. I mean, my heart… so you're sitting there and you can't hang your head any lower, and we took all this and now what… what can we do?*

Anne's struggle began internally, and her compulsion to figure out how to address the transgression became the focal point of the narrative. As is often the case, the situation snowballed and got worse before it got better. A painfully insensitive student said, "Well, they're in our country now. And it wasn't that great of a piece of art. It's our school." Anne refused to let this stand, and she strongly reprimanded the student.

> *"I'm ashamed of you." I couldn't believe that. I said, "No, no, no. We did something really wrong here." And so, while we continue to try to make reparations and to work through it with the muralist and the mural committee, I really got a sense of who my community was at that moment.*

The student actually played a very important role for Anne. Although this student was not the person who painted over the mural, he presented as someone who required Anne's attention and energy. Here was a living example of a student in need of individualized education, and Anne was all too ready to provide strongly worded guidance!

Anne told a classic story that featured some traditional components of a narrative, including an evaluation that explains the significance of the story and a coda that returns the perspective to the present, where she can engage in further reflection on the incident (Labov and Waletzky 1967).

> *And when I took over being an assistant principal I learned how to just… I wanted to learn to watch and observe, and I think I'm a good listener. Not just sort of an active listener, but I'm a good listener. But I think there comes a time when you can't just sit, and I think that my body told me that. I didn't think about it, it wasn't a decision that I was cogent of making. It was like "no more of this!"*

Anne clearly articulated her realization that a good leader must do more than listen—a good leader must take action! The questioner offered some support but also pushed for further reflection: "Good for you! And what would you do differently?" Notice Anne's authentic speech, her fragmented thoughts, the process of making sense of a difficult situation and figuring out how to move forward.

> *We made an egregious error. This was reckless disregard for a number, I mean, on many levels, on many, many levels… And I can tell you I'd never let it happen again, but I can't change that. It's heart wrenching… Oh, I would have taken it much slower. Much, much slower. I mean we… it was like moving into a house and then tearing down walls before you ever actually figured out which walls needed to come down. It was that quick… and I'm… you know I think, yeah it was just so quick. And I was, I knew, my heart… and I'm thinking, "God, I'm forty-five years old, I'm going to have a heart attack… But I think we were just doing things too quickly and trying to… chase out the ghosts.*

In this part of her narrative, Anne mentioned God, talked about having a heart attack, and then brought ghosts—the spirits of dead people—into her story. It is obvious that this situation impacted Anne to the very core of her being. Her position as a school leader compelled her to carry the weight of responsibility for the wrongs that were committed. One can safely assume that, in the future, Anne will do everything in her power to ensure that individuals under her watch will be more thoughtful and considerate; they will not be "doing things too quickly."

THE POWER OF THE WRITTEN WORD

In another equity promoter story told by a first-year elementary school principal, Antonio K. (September 2002) described a series of actions he was compelled to take to address a difficult situation. Throughout his narrative, it became clear that Antonio's actions were very much guided by a core value: all students should be treated respectfully. The story began when Antonio heard from two of his male students that the physical education teacher had chastised them in front of the class for failing to participate in the soccer lesson. According to the students, the "teacher told us we were behaving like girls, and that we needed to stop kissing." The students in the classroom readily picked up the taunting where the teacher left off, calling them "locas viejas," a derogatory, homophobic Spanish phrase.

When the teacher was confronted, he denied saying these things and maintained his story that the students were sent to the office because they were being disruptive. The students were quite clear about what had happened, and their report was in direct contrast to the teacher's version of the story. Antonio felt that he was walking a difficult line. He believed that the students' story was accurate, and that the teacher was trying to save face and avoid disciplinary action. Antonio remained committed to handling the situation so that the students would feel safe and validated; he understood his responsibility to communicate a clear expectation regarding student discipline to the teacher.

Yet Antonio understood that he could not reprimand the teacher in front of the students: "I couldn't tell the teacher [he was] lying, because I don't have any proof; however, I pushed the situation to the point where the teacher said, 'I apologize if I said something that offended you.'"

However, Antonio didn't feel that the situation was adequately resolved merely because the teacher ceded a halfhearted apology. Other school leaders may not have had the time, energy, or commitment to take on a sensitive issue such as this one, but Antonio refused to let it go. He spoke to the teacher, presenting a clear and direct message: "When we are using 'you are behaving like a girl' as a put-down, what are we saying about women? What are we saying about girls? What is the message we are giving to the kids?" But, what effect does the administrative lecture really have on students or teachers or parents? What can school leaders do to get individuals to be more mindful or sensitive about their words and actions?

In this case, Antonio felt that he needed to drive his point home and put a bit more strength behind his words—this is where written documentation can serve to heighten the intensity and seriousness of a situation. Antonio spoke to the teacher with authority: "I have everything [written down] right here. It's not in your file, but I just want you to know we have that information." This is a clear demonstration of a school leader using power and control to achieve his desired outcome.

Antonio went on to describe how emotionally charged the situation was for him. "So that night I thought about myself; I thought about these kids… I thought [about] how I would talk to this teacher first." Although this was presented as an open-ended story, it was clear that Antonio had taken charge of the situation. He had exhibited leadership and expressed his passion for playing the role of equity promoter. In the telling of this powerful story, it was evident that Antonio had risen to a new level in his role as school principal, leader, and protector of children, and the questioners offered positive, affirming remarks about the actions he had taken.

Although Antonio played the role of enforcer and made it very clear how the teacher was expected to behave on the school campus, he primarily played the role of equity promoter as a means of protecting the children under his care. He owned the role and expressed his personal values of respect, equity, and justice. This was a personal mission that he felt compelled to fulfill; Antonio was not content to let the situation be about a single teacher. He asked himself, "What have I done to really create a different kind of community within the school and different kinds of messages for gays?… I thought [about what we could] do as a school."

Antonio's story has a sense of closure, but it also offers a window into the future. The work is not done, and Antonio feels compelled to hang on to these learnings and apply them as he works to develop a more inclusive, equity-oriented school culture.

MOVING INTO THE "VICE PRINCIPALS' GHETTO"

Brianne D. (September 2004) is an African American vice principal in an urban high school. In the second line of her narrative, when she offered a description of the physical environment of her school, it became clear that her story would be about equity. Brianne underscored the fact that, when she was promoted from dean to assistant principal, her office was never moved; individuals within the community made note of this fact as well:

> *So we're in this nice, new building and all the vice principals' offices are lined up behind the principal's office. And they call it the "vice principals' ghetto." It's so funny how names get tagged in*

> *the school very quickly… And everybody said, "Oh, so you didn't move…" And I was like, "I'm not sure." Because I'm still doing discipline and safety. There's a string of offices that surround what's called the "on-campus suspension room," which I supervise… So, everybody was like, "Yeah, but you're an assistant principal. You have to move over here." So I talked to the principal about it and he said, "No, no. I think you should stay where you are." So I was like, "Okay." Well, how it got taken by the community was totally different, because there are only two African American assistant principals. We're both females. One is on her way out to retire. So people were just appalled that I hadn't moved over here. And they said, "But then why are all the other assistant principals over here and you aren't over here?"*

Brianne acknowledged that initially she didn't see the need to have her office moved with the other assistant principals. She understood that there was a functional reason for her to be in proximity of individuals and programs that she was expected to supervise. She explained, "It seemed to make sense for me to be exactly where I was, because if I was [with the other assistant principals], I would spend my time running back and forth because that's what I do. Everything I do is over there." Brianne began her story with a description of a space called the "vice principals' ghetto," which obviously carries a lot of meaning—*ghetto* is a word with strong emotional import. Brianne then included additional nicknames that allowed a glimpse into the students' and teachers' perceptions about the different spaces on campus:

> *But this place over here became known as the "big house," where I am, whereas "out in the field"… I wasn't sure how it got… it sort of came as a joke. Like, people started saying, "Oh, I'm not going over to the big house or the white house." And we're on the other side of the campus.*

The "big house" and the "white house" are where the white administrators do their work. What does it mean to be "on the other side of the campus"? This conjures up images of "living on the wrong side of the tracks," or situating a special education classroom in a portable, remote room, away from the center of the school campus. Language mirrors perception, and one school leader captured this notion with his frequent refrain: "Perception is everything!" The perception of institutional racism can become a strong motivation for educational leaders to make changes—even at the expense of function or efficiency.

> *So it had been going around among the African American staff. Because all the people I work with are black. And all the kids I deal with are black or students of color… and I hadn't said anything. I knew there had been talk… Well, the principal found out and he was so upset. Because he is a white man that works on his staff daily, hourly, minute by minute. He is an incredible human being. He was appalled. And he said, "… no one said or did anything about this." So he got so angry, he said, "I want to move you over here." He said, "I'm going to move [these two white vice principals] over there."*

Notice the strength of emotion that emerges in this narrative: "He was appalled… he got so angry." Brianne was not a decision maker in this story; nevertheless, after her promotion, she found herself right in the middle of an equity-related issue. Fortunately, as a member of a highly functional administrative team, Brianne was afforded the opportunity to weigh in on this uncomfortable situation. As Brianne explained, the team took the time to explore and address the equity issues with the support of an outside consultant who worked with their school:

> What happened was, we started having this talk among our admin. team… And he's doing this race and equity work just within our small group. It's interesting because what happens is… people say, "Yes, let's have this talk." When you say that and you have black people in the room who have lived through this, the talk… it becomes… people can't take it. They get uncomfortable. They start sweating. They turn colors because, if you start, you really want to hear the talk.

This is how the work of an equity promoter often takes place—having hard conversations in small-group settings. It is not clear from the narrative who initiated this conversation or who made the decision to bring the team together to do this kind of work, but Brianne became animated as she described the dynamic that often emerges when hard conversations take place: "They turn colors." Brianne never said what colors people turn, but it is fascinating that she described individuals as turning colors when talking about racially charged issues. After the situation began to unfold, Brianne found her voice, and she was not afraid to call the situation as she saw it:

> First it was very quiet… And I started saying, "Look at how you set up even your vice principals." I said, "You have three white men, one white woman, and the two black administrators at the end." I said, "Your other black administrator is 'in the field,' as they say." I said, "Just even looking at that, these are things that we as black people look at immediately. I noticed it immediately. But was I going to say anything? I can't say something about every single thing I see because I see things continuously. So it's like you have to learn how to choose your battles."

Brianne further contextualized the situation. She understood that the positioning of an office was just one component—one minor example of institutional racism. Yet, as an action-oriented leader, she did not want the situation to be ignored. Brianne went on to highlight additional areas that needed to be addressed, including other facilities-related issues:

> The other thing that I really wanted to come out… I felt that all of these people in the room were well meaning, but they wanted to fix everything right away. And I was like, you know what? This is 200 or 300 years that this has been going on. You need to go home. You need to reflect. You need to start thinking about it… I said, "Don't come in and go, 'We're moving to new offices and that's going to change it! Now we're being good.'"

Brianne expressed a strong commitment for her work as equity promoter, but she knew that things would not change overnight—a lot of work still needed to be done. In the conclusion to her story, she extracted herself from the situation and began to look at equity-based issues that were prevalent outside of the school community:

> *I want the team to understand… all of this stuff that we're talking about is not going to change immediately. And it's not going to change maybe even in our lifetime. But we can start… to have the conversation and reflect and ingest and digest what is happening. The way you raise your child—you have a baby. The… things you say to her, what you expose her to, how you start to… you look at things… what's on your walls at home, what you're watching on TV.*

The work of the equity promoter resides not only in the classrooms and the office of the school; it makes its way into the homes of the students. The time and the place of the work are not confined to school hours or the boundaries of the school campus. A true school leader opens the dialogue and presents problems and challenges that need fixing. An equity promoter will not likely have all of the answers, but that shouldn't prevent school leaders from engaging in the work. Singleton and Linton assert that equity-related stories and "courageous conversations" will trigger:

> *…a moral, intellectual, social, and emotional shift that allows participants to revisit their many professional development binders of previous trainings with a newly developed racial lens and language. If people expect and accept non-closure in racial discourse, then the more they talk, the more they learn; and the more they learn, the more appropriate and promising will be their actions and interventions. (2006, 65)*

A professional learning community can provide a wonderful space for new leaders to make sense of their challenging experiences and engage in proactive thinking about how best to navigate equity-related situations, but one of the critical skills that can be developed through the storytelling process is the art of *listening*—with one's heart as well as one's head. In the reflective storytelling process, listeners are expected to take in the thoughts, feelings, words, and actions of the storyteller; they are not to respond with a story of their own! They are encouraged to ask clarifying and probing questions that can help all group members deeply understand the experience of the storyteller and the core issues being shared.

It is not easy for a school leader to experience emotional transformations in the public eye, and it never feels comfortable for a leader to realize that an insensitive comment or a thoughtless mistake has negatively impacted others. However, the school leader should not feel compelled to present a polished, professional, and scripted persona to the world, in which every word and action is orchestrated. At its essence, the reflective storytelling process is all about learning to lead with authenticity and humility. As school leaders, we are all going to make mistakes. It is how we learn from these mistakes, how we come to a collective understanding about what has happened, how we acknowledge our shortcomings, and how we commit to move forward that define who we are as school leaders and human beings.

At the end of the day, an equity promoter will cultivate the conditions in which all individuals can have some of their needs for love, affection, and belonging met within the school community. According to Maslow (1943), these are some of the basic needs of all human beings. Effective leaders create the space within their professional learning communities—and in their schools—to take risks, make mistakes, tell stories, have difficult conversations, provide support and guidance, and maintain growth-oriented learning.

Reflective Questions for Prospective and Practicing School Leaders

❧ What are some of the most common equity issues that exist in your school community?

❧ What are some of the organizational systems, structures, and practices that contribute to these equity issues?

❧ What are some of the consequences that students of color face when they conform to the expectations of a white-dominated school?

❧ In what ways do you support and nurture diverse points of view?

❧ What are the forums or venues in your school that are set up to address equity issues?

❧ Do your staff members look like the student body they are serving? Does this matter? Why or why not?

❧ What is the cultural, ethnic, and racial complexion of the various committees and parent groups that are connected to your school? How has your school community reached out to underrepresented groups of parents?

❧ Have you experienced racism, sexism, or discrimination in the school setting? How did you respond?

❧ Have you ever been accused of being racist, sexist, or discriminatory? How did you respond?

❧ What does it mean to be an ally to those who have less power and opportunity than you have?

❧ What is your comfort level in having hard conversations with those who express prejudicial beliefs or engage in acts of discrimination?

❧ What does fairness look like?

❧ What is the relationship between equity and equality for you?

Chapter 5

THE SCHOOL ADMINISTRATOR AS INSTRUCTIONAL LEADER

It's a massive undertaking… It's a labor of love. But I can see that these guys want to learn. And these guys can make it. So who am I to stand back and not help these kids?… I'm looking for two things. I'm looking for the scores to go up. I'm looking to help these kids help themselves essentially. I want to see the self-esteem of the students rise when they know they can do it.

Steven G., September 2004

If education is all about the business of teaching and learning, then why did only 36 narratives (15 percent) of the 246 in our study portray school leaders actively and directly playing the role of *instructional leader*? Instructional leaders, very simply, make the hard decisions and take the necessary actions to ensure that *all* students are learning. The task can seem somewhat colossal when instructional leaders actively work to develop a professional learning community that will collaboratively address critical questions, such as those framed by DuFour, Eaker, and DuFour (2005):

- What should students know and be able to do?

- How will school communities know if they know it?

- How good is good enough?

- What will school communities do when students don't learn?

- What will school communities do if students have already learned it?

The intersection of curriculum, assessment, and instruction can be a very complicated and contentious throughway to student learning. Prompting changes in teacher practice is a formidable challenge for even the most passionate of school leaders. The resistance to school reform that exists in most schools creates a long road from the principal's office to the student's desk. The assumption that the principal's actions can influence the teachers' practice—which in turn will result in increased student learning—requires much more than a leap of faith. The structural isolation of classrooms, the desire for autonomy among teachers, and the transience of many administrators make it difficult to implement new systems, structures, or practices (to improve student learning) with any kind of fidelity (Meyer and Rowan 1977).

Indeed, many teachers actively resist instructional oversight and accountability. Teacher unions have fought hard to prevent the linking of teacher evaluations, or even merit pay, to student achievement. Researchers face tremendous challenges in proving causal relationships between teacher actions and student learning, but clearly the relationship between student and teacher is the most important one that exists in the school community. The challenge for the instructional leader is how to influence teacher practice.

When we reviewed the aggregate of administrative narratives, an interesting finding emerged: of the 246 narratives, there were only 5 (2 percent) teacher supporter narratives. This data begs the question "With whom is the school leader aligned?" A common assumption might be that new leaders, who often were schoolteachers themselves prior to becoming administrators, very naturally would align themselves with the teachers they are charged with overseeing. However, after unpacking the administrative narratives, it is clear that the primary compulsion of the novice school leader is to play many different roles—especially variations of the *child advocate*. In other words, school leaders readily relegate their previous alliances with teachers to a secondary position: children do come first!

This new alliance is not lost on those who make the transition from teacher to principal in the same school. Roland Barth, a well-respected researcher/former principal, shares his perception of this metamorphosis:

> *Then something happens. In only a few months principals are transformed—not by choice, design, or wish—from teacher advocates to teacher adversaries. Something with the peculiar culture of schools and school systems converts good intentions into bad relationships and changes colleagues into superordinates and subordinates. Something in the alchemy of schools contorts friends who would help teachers into administrators who require more and tolerate less. The teacher who becomes principal emerges from the chrysalis a different species. (Barth 1990, 21)*

Of course, there are many reasons why dramatic changes may take place in the perspectives, priorities, actions, and efforts of school leaders when they move into the world of administration. As the following stories show, it may not be such a bad thing that our school leaders "require more and tolerate less." Even when administrators have a powerful conviction that the education of our young people should come first, many obstacles stand in the way of becoming an effective instructional leader.

The scholarly writings on school leadership development regularly include discussion of the importance of instructional leadership, but little actual training has been provided on how to make the leap from theory to action. Richard Elmore eloquently summarizes this quandary:

> *Instructional leadership is the equivalent of the Holy Grail in educational administration. Most programs that prepare superintendents and principals claim to be in the business of training the next generation of instructional leaders... This is mainly just talk. In fact few administrators of any kind or at any level are directly involved with instruction. (2000, 9)*

The role of the principalship has evolved over the years, becoming more political, more bureaucratic, and more weighed down by legal mandates and the immense responsibility of pushing paper—all of which impedes the ability to serve as an effective instructional leader. According to Doug Reeves in

Assessing Educational Leaders (2004), 71 percent of principals strongly agreed that they should manage their time to be an instructional leader; however, only 45 percent said that they did so. Evelyn N. (November 2004)—a new elementary school principal—expressed the overwhelming feelings that new school leaders often experience:

> My first month of school I would have almost cried. I just really wanted to break down and cry simply because it was just so overwhelming. And I think more than anything I was just exhausted. I was working 12, 14 hours a day. My average is nothing less than 10. Those strong emotions came out of me because I felt myself doing the very best job that I could, but at the same time I was angry and frustrated with myself because I knew I wasn't getting done the level of work that I wanted to, simply because I didn't have the brain cells left to do it. I didn't have the physical strength to do it, and I was sleeping probably about three, four hours a night and getting up and getting to work at 7, 6:30. Starting that same vicious cycle over and over again. I'm trying to find a medium and a balance between all of the things that go on in the day-to-day life of being an administrator.

Over time, expert principals become more adept at separating the urgent from the important. Additionally, they will have spent a significant amount of time building an effective and efficient school organization whereby all stakeholders understand the norms and expectations. According to Pepperl and Lezotte (2004), efficient principals are interrupted (or allow themselves to be interrupted) half as often as their more typical counterparts (however, their reported rates of interruption—2.5 percent, compared with the typical 5.2 percent—seem particularly low based on my own observation and experience). The work of many school leaders seems to move from one interruption to the next. Prior to the advent of high-stakes testing and increasing legal and bureaucratic demands, Goldsborough noted that "the apparent relentless erosion of his function as educational leader is a trend of the utmost concern to principals... It is quite obvious that many principals feel themselves succumbing to the increasing welter of paperwork and non-educational administrivia" (1971, 36).

THE CONFINEMENT OF HIGH STANDARDS

The following story describes the specific challenge of keeping student learning at the forefront of the work in an alternative school, but the challenge of maintaining a strong instructional focus exists in elementary, middle, and high schools; urban and suburban schools; and large and small schools alike. Jack K. (November 2003)—a continuation high school principal—provided an overview of the extraordinary challenges he faced and the overwhelming context of his work as an instructional leader:

> Lately, continuation high school has become one of the most depressing places on Earth... Kids are shooting themselves up in a rather fast and furious pace right now. For example, one day they brought in the kid that shot the other kid on the bus... And, they ended up catching this guy who shot

this girl through the door [of her own home]… so he was there, too. And it just throws this incredible amount of tension at the school. It really affected me. I was really not in denial of what these kids do and what they're capable of, but I never really thought about it that much because it was just my school and I'm just going to worry about teaching and learning… I didn't talk to anybody about this. It was something I was internalizing myself and didn't really think that perhaps the teachers that have to deal with these kids all day long might have the same reaction.

It would be quite understandable and appropriate for a school leader to focus simply on discipline, safety, order, and compliance under such circumstances. But if school leaders are to provide our young people with an opportunity to be successful in college or the workplace, they have an urgent responsibility to equip their students with the necessary skills and knowledge to think critically and compete with other students who may have enjoyed more robust learning experiences. Although educators must attend to the social, emotional, and ethical development of their students, academic achievement needs to be a primary goal. Instructional leaders are charged with creating the structures necessary to support an academic focus:

Then the first day we come back, it's staff development. So I had this lengthy morning program that I was going to go to the teachers with. One was reviewing some of the data that we received from the state, which was problematic because the month before the test, we didn't have any of the kids that were there on the day of the test.

Even with a strong resolve to focus on the improvement of teaching and learning activities and to use data to inform instruction, challenges will exist. Never are the data as clean as we would like them to be. Never is the assessment perfectly aligned with the standards. Never are the testing conditions as ideal as we hope. In this particular situation, the teachers had very little time to actually teach the students who were being assessed. Although alternative education programs tend to be a highly transitory place for students, Jack did not accept excuses. Rather, he acknowledged the reality of the data set he was working with:

These are the kids you had at your school and this is how they performed. I made sure the teachers understood that, that this is how I was approaching this, but that we do have other indicators and assessments that show that the state data were pretty close to the kind of kids we serve. That they're far-below-basic kids. One way to help these kids was to concentrate on the standards. Immediately, I got this reaction from the teaching staff that "I don't know our kids" and that if I knew our kids, I wouldn't be telling them to teach standards-based instruction.

It may be easy to dismiss this example as atypical of teachers' beliefs and expectations in more traditional public schools, but it is shocking how frequently school leaders in *all* settings describe the challenge of confronting low expectations. This is often the starting point for the work of an instructional leader.

> *I noticed that the science teacher didn't have standards-based [materials]… The other teachers just don't have a clue. So it became pretty clear to me as I was talking to these people that they haven't learned the standards, so they're arguing this stuff that they know nothing about. That's basically what I said to them. "If you really knew [the standards], you probably wouldn't find it so offensive"… The reality is there's nothing in those standards that's offensive. And that if teachers embraced standards a long time ago, we wouldn't be in this high-stakes [place] surrounding the assessment that we're in right now. The teachers were obviously upset about this, so I dropped it.*

After Jack shared his initial diagnosis of the problem, he described the emotional state of the teachers and made a decision to "drop it." This was not necessarily a bad decision. Sometimes it can be counterproductive to continue pushing when there is extreme resistance. Changes in beliefs and practice take time, and it may be better to conduct professional learning in a one-on-one situation. But the formal professional development continued:

> *Then we went on to the blackboard configuration—which I mandated—that no teacher is doing. I decided I was going to do a lesson for the teachers on their culture development teaching strategies. I did a blackboard configuration. I started with a "do now." We did the whole thing. I showed how long it took me to put the lesson on the board. It took about two minutes. The hardest part was for me to write out the question that they were supposed to answer. All these grunts and groans about this. The funny thing is I heard the same reaction from [the high-performing high school in which I worked], where 90 percent of the kids are Asian. Well, at our school, all we have are African American kids.*

Jack was being extremely reflective regarding the challenges he faced. He continued his work as an instructional leader and toward the development of clear and consistent standards-based instruction. Interestingly, he did not end his professional development with a focus on academics:

> *I closed up the staff development; we'd been there for a few hours. I decided to end it by talking about general policy procedures that a supervising counselor asked me to remind the teachers of. One teacher was very upset and [the concern was communicated as an accusation that I was] an administrator who doesn't protect them from this evil force… This one teacher who initially started the conversation was almost yelling at me and interrupting me. For the first time since I'd been at that school in front of the faculty I lost my temper… I pointed my finger at him and said, "I'm going to finish what I have to say!" And everyone went quiet. Then I said, "Obviously people are upset about certain issues. My suggestion is that you write them down. If you want me to do something about addressing certain issues you have, I will be happy to do everything I can. We all know that things are complicated; it's a political minefield." So that ended things.*

So much for ending a professional development on a positive and productive note with a strong academic focus. No wonder that many school leaders, novice and experienced alike, bemoan the fact that the operational/managerial component of their work regularly supersedes the work that is most important. Jack continued reflecting on his work as an instructional leader:

> " *I was a little upset and it wasn't until a couple of days later that I thought, "I bet none of this was directed toward me." There is this certain type of ebb and flow where teachers, at every school… sometimes they're really positive and everything's working fine and then all of a sudden, it seems like the whole faculty is really down and discouraged. But then it flows back.* "

During the questioning phase of the storytelling process, Jack's colleagues asked him to dig a little deeper about his emotions and intentions, especially in response to his description of one of the teachers as "a snake waiting to pounce." Jack shared his initial reaction: "My number one goal was to get those people out of my face. We're done with this meeting, everybody go to lunch!" But after some additional probing questions, Jack pulled back the curtain and revealed his underlying motivation and beliefs:

> " *Part of it was, I had been going to this workshop on raising achievement for African American kids. You go to it on a Saturday and drag yourself there. Once you're there, you're thinking, "I gotta keep doing this stuff."… Perhaps [this anger] wasn't all directed toward me and the decisions I make… Adult learning theory isn't really that different than teaching kids. Sometimes you have to use scaffolding to take people where you want them to go. And you think just because they have college degrees and master's degrees that you can hit them over the head with things, and it doesn't work.* "

When Jack was asked about what his next steps were going to be, he offered that it might be best to back off a little bit before pressing on with his moral imperative to maintain a strong focus on instruction. He confidently explained: "We're going to have a party… to decompress things." It is not uncommon for an instructional leader to take one step backward after taking two steps forward. However, Jack never gave any indication that he would give up his focus on academic achievement for all students.

ARBITRARY ACCESS TO HONORS CLASSES

Lest the reader believe that the challenges of serving as an instructional leader are unique to alternative schools, meet Mark C. (May 2003), a high school assistant principal who began his story by sharing one of his primary goals: "I've been trying to create a focus on student achievement and [I've been] trying to create opportunities for more students to have access to a more rigorous curriculum." Mark provided the context for his story by describing district initiatives, weighted GPA, and access to challenging courses:

> *[This] led me then to take a closer look at what were the existing practices… So who gets into these honors sections is what I started to take a look at. In the sciences and in the math class it's sequential, and foreign languages, too. It's pretty much how you take them, the sequence. There's not a lot of discussion there. If you're in your fourth year of Spanish, it's automatically an AP class you're in. If you've gotten into pre-calculus, well, then you show up at AP calculus… However, the issue is in English. In our English curriculum, we have honors classes freshman year, honors class sophomore year… but junior and senior years you [get the extra grade point average]… And what I found out is that they have a quota system. The quota system was pretty much based on the number of sections that this department wanted to offer. So it didn't have anything to do with a student's ability… So they were capping the total.*

Mark didn't set out to discover the ways in which the English department denied access to students who wanted to enroll in the English honors class. Sometimes, long-standing practices are exposed in the most unexpected ways:

> *And I uncovered this kind of accidentally, because all of a sudden I heard there was going to be a list that was going to be posted and only the kids on the list were going to be allowed in. In fact, the data clerk was telling me that every year she gets the list and then she pulls all of the kids out of honors classes if they're not on this magic list… and it was disjointed, it wasn't alphabetized, and they had these scores that were supposedly based on some sort of assessments, a writing test they had done, a reading test they had taken, teacher recommendation. I don't know, they had some sort of formula, which I have to admit, was not too impressive, but I didn't even bother to fully analyze it because I just didn't believe in it at all.*

Here, Mark began to strongly, although indirectly, reveal his underlying values: he wanted students to have greater access to the more rigorous curriculum—or the extra grade point average, which can be extremely significant for college-bound students.

> *And then I looked at how many students had signed up, and over 130 students had signed up. So we were talking about bumping out close to 40 kids from this honors class. And so I said, "Wow, that's a big discrepancy here… 130 kids have signed up. How are we going to kick these kids out?" And then I started going, wait a minute, I can run a report that [shows] grade distribution by course. So I can see how many As and Bs there were in the different classes. And imagine this, in our honors section classes alone, there were 107 students who got an A or a B. So, if you just use common sense, none of these formulas and assessments and tests… if a student gets an A or a B in the freshman honors class, why shouldn't they be allowed to continue?… So where did the 90 come from?*

It is one thing to become cognizant of a problem, but it requires another skill set to move toward resolution of the problem. In this particular situation, the actions Mark took involved exposing not only that the ways of doing business were unfair and inequitable, but that they may have had long-term implications about a student's self-worth and opportunities to gain acceptance to certain colleges. Then, of course, he also faced the challenge of dealing with strong emotion:

> *I confronted the department chair. I go, "How can you tell me there's only 90 slots when there's over 90 kids who got an A or a B in the existing honors class, and there's 37 students who got an A?" And it was pretty sad. The reaction was… they felt like they had been exposed… And it had been going on for twenty years… She pretty much completely backpedaled once the data was put before her… I did inform her that at a minimum there's 144 students who definitely have rights, so we're not going to be placing any lists and so forth.*

At this point in the storytelling process, Mark became rather animated. He clearly was emboldened by the whole process and felt that this small discovery was the start of a much larger movement to open access and improve equity throughout the school system. Mark was like an investigative reporter who just broke a big story and was eager to share the news with a wider audience:

> *I called the superintendent; he was all fired up. He couldn't believe how outrageous it was as well. I called an open meeting for the English department; I'd already told them I wanted to talk to them about this and what I wanted to talk to them about. So we'll see what happens Monday, but we're going to go through this process. So it was just pretty fascinating, and it's also kind of interesting using the technologies… for data-driven decision making… One of the things I felt good about was bringing the whole group together and making the process more transparent.*

Toward the end of the reflective storytelling process—and with prodding from his colleagues—Mark softened his stance a little bit and began to contemplate the profound responsibility he had to provide feedback and facilitate change as an instructional leader. Even when school leaders are doing the right thing, the political risks and the impact on relationships throughout the school community can be enormous:

> *I started to get weak. I mean, usually I'm pretty loud; sometimes I'm a little too boisterous. I actually saw myself starting to backpedal. It was uncomfortable; I'll be honest with you. And usually I'm pretty confident, and maybe can feel tough, but then when I've got this person who's been teaching for twenty-something years, I know she's a really good teacher, I like her as a person, and as a first-year administrator I'm telling her "you may be able to get away with this, but I'm not going to allow it." And I was in that position and I didn't want to use the "I"; I wanted to explain why. And so I was caught where I didn't want to be so forceful because I wanted, in the moment, to tell her her business, but then I worried about the mutiny and the relationships, and really if they stop respecting your work and working*

with you, it can be hell. But at the same time I knew I was right. And I said that I felt that I was right. So how do you push forward without alienating and causing the staff to rebel? But then you know that it's good for kids and you know it's not harming anybody… I didn't want the conflict, I didn't want the confrontation. But I stuck with it. **99**

Here is a school leader who is beginning to understand that, just because he is right, his job will not necessarily be easy and he will not always have the full support of the staff as he embarks on the journey of instructional leadership. This narrative also shows how the roles of the school leader regularly overlap and do not always fit into neat categories. Although Mark primarily was committed to improving the instructional program of the school as a whole and affording more rigorous opportunities to more students, he simultaneously had to play the roles of system builder and enforcer. To achieve his desired outcomes, Mark was forced to operate in several different spaces and intervene with many different stakeholders within the school community.

PURPLE FOLDERS AND BLACK STUDENTS

There are times when an instructional leader may feel profound passion and personal commitment to change the way educators organize their work and think about the students they teach. The school leader who shared the following story is an African American woman working with a predominantly white staff. Robin F. (November 2003) began her narrative by providing the larger context for her work before narrowing in on her area of focus. Robin is exceptionally fluent with the demographics and other key data points in her school:

66 *I am academic coordinator at [my] school and I'm new in this position… My main goal and my main duties at my site are to monitor and promote the achievement of the underachievers. I deal with students of color, which is a dominant force at our school, like 90 percent—English language learners, etc. I do this various ways. I am very heavily involved in classrooms. We have thirty-six classrooms going at one time. We're year-round. So we have four tracks. We have approximately fifty-three teachers. It's a K–6 school, and we have 996 students at this point. Our enrollment has dropped. We were at 1,036 last year. This is my second year there. Last year I spent the year getting familiar with things. I was very much an observer, and now I'm ready to dig in and begin my work.* **99**

Robin soon began to talk about not only the focus of her work but also the means by which she organized members of her school community to address an obvious achievement gap.

66 *I'm starting a group called "Sticky Issues" and this is going to be an introduction to that. The first sticky issue that we're going to deal with is the achievement of African American students. African American students at this point are about 27 percent represented at our school. Last year it was more,*

33 percent. A lot of them are moving [out of the community]. Tonight we're going to be talking about the history of our schools. I have to delve into the history of the district, which at one point was predominantly white. And that's changing very fast. At our site, we have 84 percent white teachers.

Notice how Robin provided a rationale for the work she was doing. Even though the largest subgroup in her school comprised English language learners, Robin pointed out that no resources or programs were in place to support the learning of African American students.

The reason I wanted to focus on African American achievement is because in one subject they don't have a support system in place. English language learners have a support system. They have resources of people and they have programming and they have money. We have what's called "bilingual associates" and they go to the classrooms. They do parent communications and they work directly with the students and they're there all day, every day. Of our African American students, 47 percent of them are achieving below basic and far below basic in those two categories. They are put into what is called a "purple folder system," where teachers are to document what interventions they provide to those students in the classroom. That was my main focus last year, and pretty much my experience was that teachers don't like to do the purple folders. It's another piece of work that they don't feel they need to do.

The school had a system in place whereby underachieving students were identified; the onus of responsibility was on teachers to come up with specific interventions and document them in the purple folders. Robin did not believe that this was a well-supported program to deal with underperforming students. Rather, it sounds as though teachers were expected to work alone, while administrators were expected to monitor and hold teachers accountable—which can understandably feel like a game of "gotcha!" to the teachers in the school community.

My challenge was for them to look at the purple folder in a different way. And to also see that in our changing times the brunt of the responsibility falls on their shoulders. [We spent a lot of time talking about] differentiation; we talked about that so much we're really actually doing it. And looking at the individual needs of each and every student in your class… So I opened [the Sticky Issues Committee] up to the staff, and I've gotten very mixed reviews. Some people are really looking forward to the meeting. I have a core group… out of the fifty teachers, I have a core group of three teachers, the vice principal, myself, and our intervention provision specialist, who really serves as a social counselor.

Although her story did not present as a linear progression of problem-solving, Robin identified some instructional strategies—differentiation and individualization—and she pulled together a core group of individuals who were interested in working on this challenging issue. The Sticky Issues team had only five committed adults, but an effective instructional leader will start with a core group of interested individuals and build on their collective efforts, one step at a time. But even eager and committed volunteers can be tentative when stepping into an arena with issues of race and equity.

> *We just had a meeting yesterday. At last week's meeting, we were sitting in a room and it was brought to my attention that the staff members needed my permission to help students with their language, with their oral language and their written language. Because they did not feel comfortable correcting, as they put it, black students… I said, "You're the coach. Can you do the writing piece?" She said, "No, I can't, because it has to come from you. I cannot tell them that when they hear an African American student using African American speech. You have to help them with that and tell them that that's not standard English. It has to come from you."*

As the team jumped into the work, different instructional needs came into focus. The team realized the importance of having the African American students learn standard English; however, they felt that only Robin, an African American educator, could provide this kind of professional development. Next came the resistance that often emerges when the magnitude of the challenges are brought to the surface:

> *Some people began to tell me that maybe I shouldn't focus on that. There are only 27 percent now; the numbers have dropped. We're really talking about a language issue. Maybe you should talk about the Hispanic population instead because it's 47 percent… The principal said, "Maybe we can talk about both groups." People started trying to twist what was going to happen.*

But Robin held her ground, and she obviously understood the importance of maintaining a clear focus. She also refused to position herself as the authority. Rather, she empowered the group to grapple with the "sticky issues" and to determine their own set of best practices:

> *I was pretty adamant about, "No. This is our focus for this time. If others want to start another group and have another focus group, I think this would be a good thing." Some teachers went to them and said this is a new way of looking at things. They had never been allowed to have a dialogue. I'm allowing time for them to sit in small groups, talk about different things about instructing African American students, share those out, come back and actually come up with some strategies. Plot where everybody's concerns are. We're going to record this. Then actually leave with some ideas that we shared.*

Many professional educators are uncomfortable playing the role of expert when they address issues of race and equity. At the conclusion of the storytelling process, Robin shared some of her personal reflections about the weight of working through these issues. However, she remained steadfast in her determination to address these important issues head-on:

> *It's just been very interesting. I felt at some point I was trying to be set up for failure, because the ideas given to me were like "you should do this" or "you should do that." I'm really nervous about the meeting, but I feel confident and I'm grateful that I have enough prior knowledge to be able to keep my focus, and I didn't deter from that because that's where people were trying to take me. I'm hearing now*

that people are really against the meeting. They hope that we don't have to look at any more data. I've heard comments like, "Oh, they wanted us to do Black History Month and now we've got to talk about black children"… It's a very delicate subject, and I'm affected and I'm worried. 99

Even though Robin remained deeply focused on the academic achievement of a subgroup of students in her school, as in Mark's story, she played a multiplicity of roles. In this particular case, it was impossible to separate the work of an instructional leader from that of an equity promoter. The language, actions, and desired outcomes very much overlap.

ISSUES WITH AUTHORITY

As a school leader, a lot of the important work needs to be done one-on-one with targeted individuals. Although organizational systems, structures, and lines of authority exist, an effective instructional leader will be most concerned with changing the practices that take place within the confines of a classroom—and some of the most significant conversations need to take place with the most resistant and oppositional teachers. Amanda T. (October 2003)—a new middle school principal—described just such a challenge:

I was very uncomfortable the other day. I have a teacher who is clearly anti-authority. So anything an authority figure says, he's going to disagree with it because an authority figure said it. Clearly, he does not like women, so if you put a woman in authority, now we've got a problem. He has, on more than one occasion, said [to me] that I'm only making this decision because that's what the powers-that-be tell me to do and that I don't have [a will] of my own. He's extremely confrontational all the time… He's very, very unhappy, ultimately a very scared little boy, but that's hard to say to somebody. 99

As all good storytellers do, Amanda provided the context of her story. She painted a picture—not using a physical description of the teacher she was working with, but by illuminating the internal landscape of the teacher. Then she launched into the area of conflict. As is often the case, there was more than one area of concern:

We are now in the tenth week of school. He has yet to submit any of the lesson plans that have been requested of him. Oftentimes he misses meetings: we have grade-level meetings, we have curriculum meetings, we have literacy meetings, and we have planning time from 8 to 9. So I wrote him a memo. It wasn't even a reprimand.

I wrote: "It has come to my attention that you still haven't turned in your curriculum map; we don't have your lesson plan. We'd like to see your lesson plans for the next nine weeks." I wrote about missing a particular meeting and that he [wouldn't] get paid. 99

It is not at all unusual for individuals to respond with emotional intensity when concerns are placed in writing; never mind that these same concerns may have been communicated verbally on a number of different occasions by a number of different administrators. Most educators (most human beings!) do not like confrontation, but dealing with angry and confrontational students, teachers, and parents is a vitally important skill set that new school leaders must acquire.

> *He comes into my office and stands there. I say, "Why don't you have a seat." He says, "No." It's a power play that he is going to stand over me. And he's already taller than me and bigger than me, so I'm a little uncomfortable. He hands me the memo and says, "So this is how we are going to communicate. This is how we're going to communicate." I say, "Well, that's one way that we can communicate." He says, "Have you even checked the binder to see if my curriculum map is in there?" I say, "I was told that it was not in there. I'm going to check to verify that it's not in there, because I did see some of your paperwork, which was just the chapter header from the social studies book. I'm not sure what that is. Is that your lesson plan? Is that your curriculum map?" He just literally took the book and retyped the chapter header. I was surprised that he didn't just photocopy it.*

A little internal sarcasm may be acceptable... especially if it remains unspoken. However, it is rarely effective as a means of modifying behavior in students or teachers. As Robin shared in the previous story, when individuals find themselves in uncomfortable situations, they dodge and weave; they change the subject; they become masters of diversion and subversion. But even when Amanda was faced with aggressive behavior, she did not back down or get sidetracked:

> *So he's going through the memo and he's picking out each thing. He says, "When you talk about missing a meeting, I was on the yard. Where were you?" I say, "I was in a meeting where I was supposed to be. And you weren't." He says, "Yeah, and I never see you in the yard." I say, "Don't intimidate me. You weren't supposed to be on the yard. I don't know why you were on the yard." He says, "All of this is petty stuff. I'm doing a good job here and you're just picking at these petty little things. We have bigger issues to worry about." I say, "I think teaching is a big issue."*

Amanda's ability to focus on the primary issue at hand—his teaching—is powerful. After more back-and-forth arguments and accusations, Amanda felt compelled to pull out the "I'm in charge" card. Although this is not the ideal way to modify human behavior, there are times when a school leader must set limits and enforce them with position and power:

> *He has gotten to this place where he has to try to intimidate me. And I say, "You can't talk to me like that. I need your curriculum map, I need your lesson plans, and I need you to go to meetings, bottom line. Whether you like it or not, I'm your boss and this is what I request of you."*

Like the plot in any good horror movie, the villain would not just fade away and die. The bad guys keep coming back, struggling desperately to conquer the hero. It is surprising how often these same themes and patterns appear in the stories that new school leaders tell:

> *He walks out of my office and he comes back three seconds later. He says, "We've got a student out there, doesn't have a collared shirt on, got his belt in his hand and what are you doing? You're sitting in your office!" I say, "I was just in a meeting with you... When you saw the boy, did you say something to him?" He says, "Well, what are you doing? What are you doing?!" I say, "You need to go."*

Just as Robin simultaneously played the role of instructional leader and equity promoter, in this story, Amanda strove to play the role of instructional leader but ultimately recognized the need to play the role of enforcer. Amanda reflected on the discipline system at her school before returning to her focus on holding the teacher accountable for quality teaching.

> *I'm at this point where I'm trying to figure out how to keep him working with the kids, as minimal as it is. While maybe it's good that he probably should not be on staff next year. There's a fine dance that you do when you're not really being picky about certain things, and yet those are the kinds of things you can really document. How do you document that he does not teach standards [when] he's not up for evaluation this year?*

It was obvious that Amanda would not let go. She had identified an individual who was ineffective as a teacher and acted as a bully as well. Rather than avoid the confrontation, Amanda continued the unpleasant task of holding him accountable for all of his professional responsibilities, especially teaching.

As school leaders become cognizant of an instructional challenge (or an ineffective teacher) that they would like to take on, they often are met with extraordinary resistance. It doesn't always matter that the observations and evidence scream for something to be done. Ineffective educators who have lasted in the profession have seen their share of school reform efforts come and go:

> *The motivational challenge is particularly thorny in schools where tenured teachers have watched wave after wave of educational "reform," and skepticism abounds. New practices are often championed by transitory political powers, new school boards and legislatures bring ever-shifting directions. And all the while, the reality that educators confront becomes more difficult and not amenable to quick fixes. (Mohrman and Lawlor 1996, 117)*

The intensity of the resistance, the organizational barriers, and the lack of resources can present as insurmountable challenges to an instructional leader. It's much easier to attend to the e-mails, handle discipline, and manage the operations of the school than to deeply engage in the more important—and more complex—instructional issues. A professional learning community can provide a space for school leaders to explore best practices in a supportive environment, and hearing the stories of other colleagues can allow school leaders to realize that the problems and personalities they confront are not that unique. Other leaders have persevered and achieved desirable outcomes.

Again, reflective storytelling creates an opportunity for school leaders to better conceptualize the challenges they face. Rather than simply reacting to the stimuli in the school environment that so often present as an emergency, the storytelling process can prompt school leaders to frame what has happened and offer an analysis about why things have come to be the way they are. The stories that new leaders tell rarely are complete; they seldom offer closure. The work stories of the instructional leader can be likened to an early winter traveler hiking through the snowy wilderness: there are often unseen dangers, running water may not readily freeze, and it is quite dangerous—especially when traveling alone—to plunge a boot or an entire body into an icy cold river. Some travelers carry a stick to test the ice. They tap on the frozen waters and listen carefully for any indication of what lies below. Those individuals move slowly and methodically through uncharted territories, but those with experience travel in groups with ropes and fire-making equipment. A professional learning community can provide the essential tools and support that enable school leaders to reach their destination safely—with all students, teachers, parents, and support providers in tow.

Much has been written in the last two decades about the importance of cultivating positive self-esteem in our young people. Maslow (1943) argues that esteem is one of the highest levels in a human being's hierarchy of needs. But esteem doesn't just happen; it can't merely be given or gifted to our children. I would argue that esteem is earned from working hard, overcoming challenges, and getting things done. A primary goal for those connected with schools—students, teachers, parents, and school leaders—is student achievement, and this typically doesn't happen by chance. It comes from collaborative efforts: identifying gap areas, aligning resources, implementing strategic practices, focusing on desired outcomes, monitoring progress, and making adjustments. An effective instructional leader works collaboratively, adopts an inquiry stance, learns from unintended outcomes, and continually moves forward with new information and learnings.

Reflective Questions for Prospective and Practicing School Leaders

- Why did you become a teacher in the first place?

- How much time do you spend on instruction in your current position?

- How much time should you spend on instruction?

- How often do you allow yourself to be interrupted or distracted from instructional matters to attend to perceived crises?

- What practices should you give up (or do less of) in order to spend more time on instruction?

- What systems and structures in your school community ensure a focus on teaching and learning?

- What data do you collect to support youself in your role as an instructional leader? How do you use these data?

- How many hours each week do teachers have to collaborate around instructional matters? Are there expectations for the ways in which teachers use their collaborative work time?

- How do you respond when you come across an individual in your school who does not believe that a certain group of students can learn?

- What is the best way to get teachers to improve in the art and science of teaching?

- What organizational structures are necessary to ensure effective teaching and learning in every classroom?

- What are some of the instructional reforms that you have had difficulty embracing?

- What steps do you take when you learn that a group of students is not meeting with academic success?

Part II

SCHOOL LEADERSHIP:
The Intersection of Decisions, Values, and Emotions

When considering the various roles that school leaders play, it is important to note that they sometimes choose a particular role because their guiding principles compel them toward action; other times, they play a role because it falls clearly within their job description; and sometimes they are pressured by different stakeholder groups to play a particular role. But how does a school leader settle on which role to play? What decision-making processes do school leaders typically use? How do personal values and external influences inform their decisions? How do new leaders navigate the intense emotion that regularly accompanies their work?

Chapters 6, 7, and 8 explore the ways that participation in reflective storytelling can prompt school leaders to consider deeply their reactions, choices, and courses of action, and help them integrate new experiences. Chapter 6 begins by examining the field in which school leaders are expected to operate. I explore the human and institutional influences on their practice and present a tool designed to expose underlying priorities; I also show how the decisions and actions of school leaders are an expression of their personal and professional values.

Chapter 7 offers a detailed analysis of effective (and ineffective) decision making; in this chapter, I show how the metacognitive processes of new school leaders can impact the outcomes of their actions and contribute to their feelings of efficacy. In analyzing the stories of new school leaders, I present a metacognitive decision-making flowchart that can be used by school leaders to increase their reflective thinking and help them become more mindful as they make difficult decisions and solve complex problems.

Chapter 8 explores the triggers to intense emotion and highlights the ways that new leaders react and respond to the emotional intensity that often accompanies their decision making. I offer a graphical representation of these triggers that can serve as a framework to help new leaders predict the kinds of situations that are likely to produce internal or external angst, anger, and uncertainty. At the end of each chapter, I offer probing questions that prospective and practicing leaders might consider as they make decisions, solve problems, and work to get things done in their school communities.

Finally, Chapter 9 examines the process of identity formation in new school leaders; in this chapter, I show how new leaders who actively engage in reflective storytelling within a professional learning community can take part in deep analysis of their role playing, sensemaking, and "meaningful-making." Moving out of the classroom and into the role of the school leader is not an easy transition, but matters of the head, hands, and heart can be integrated as new site administrators learn to assume their new identity. The participants wear the cape of leadership on their school campuses every day; the reflective storytelling process provides an opportunity to examine who they are becoming and how comfortably the clothes of leadership are worn. A reflective school leader will continually consider the following questions:

- Who am I as a school leader?

- How can I learn to navigate this wildly complex environment and its conflicting goals, expectations, and desires?

- How can I meet the various expectations and role responsibilities while staying true to my own core principles?

- How can I provide the appropriate balance of support and pressure to ensure that all members of the school community are continuously learning, growing, and thriving?

Chapter 6

VALUES IN SCHOOL LEADERSHIP:
A Field of Pressures, Priorities, and Principles

Value conflicts become particularly apparent when administrator perspectives run across the organizational boundaries that traditionally separated community from school, school from district office, and district office from department or ministry... This is a more open, but less trusting environment.

Paul Thomas Begley, 1999

When a school administrator makes a decision to help a child who has skinned her knee on the schoolyard, that school leader is choosing to disregard—at least for a period of time—other roles, responsibilities, and objectives. Whenever a decision is made, a priority is set: the needs of one group of stakeholders are being met while the needs of another group are being neglected. One group may enjoy access to scarce resources, whereas another group must do without. With each decision that is made, someone or something is being valued more highly than someone or something else. As Willower and Licata argue, "Above all, administration is concerned about values. Values can be defined as conceptions of the desirable, and administrators regularly make choices from among competing conceptions of the desirable" (1997, 1).

Values also have been defined as the criteria employed in selecting goals of behavior (Davis 1949). I believe, however, that this definition requires some modification. Goals of behavior are less meaningful and important than the actual *actions* taken to achieve them. Stated values can be wildly different from values that are expressed in the form of action. The act of evaluating worth or importance is what school leaders do every day, sometimes consciously and deliberately, and sometimes unconsciously—almost automatically. When the word *value* is used in this book, its meaning extends beyond the rhetoric of the school leader and considers the most salient influence(s) in the decision-making/action-taking processes of school leaders.

Nonroutine administrative decisions require judgments about competing values and courses of action. Making such judgments is a major and continuing aspect of administration, whether the decisions are made unilaterally or collaboratively. Reflective methods, such as those elicited in the storytelling process, can be crucial to better understanding and weighing the ethical issues that regularly cross a school leader's desk. Simply deciding which problems are worthy of attention and action can become a problem in and of itself (Willower 1994). Nonetheless, finding the time for reflection and thoughtful consideration is essential for clarifying what is truly important to the school leader and the school community.

Of course, a decision maker's scope and perspective on any given topic will be limited, the range of choices overwhelming, and the possible consequences impossible to consider. Although decision makers must contend with their "bounded rationality" (March and Simon 1958), they still are expected to make decisions based on the information at hand. We have become much more data driven in our decision making, sometimes obsessed with the gathering of relevant, reliable, and valid information; yet, in 1945, Simon reminded us that "no amassing of knowledge about how the world really is can, entirely by itself, tell us how the world ought to be" (69).

For the school leader who operates in the field, a myriad of influences emerge and compete for attention and scarce resources. These groups and considerations make up the noise, or static, that permeates the educational environment. Before one can understand how a school leader makes decisions, one must understand the perspective of the various stakeholders and constituencies with whom the principal decision maker must contend. Each of the individuals and groups has its own set of beliefs and values and will often attempt to influence the decisions of a school leader.

EXPLICATION OF STAKEHOLDER DECISION-MAKING INFLUENCES

Following is an overview of the various stakeholders that saturate the world of the school leader; these were identified by looking at the stressors, tensions, and influences described in the narratives of new school leaders and corroborated by my own experience working as a teacher and administrator in various school communities. The ways in which competing beliefs and values are played out have been described as the *micropolitics* of an organization:

> *Micropolitics refers to the use of formal and informal power by individuals and groups to achieve their goals in organizations. In large part, political actions result from perceived differences between individuals and groups, coupled with the motivation to use power to influence and/or protect... Both cooperative and conflictive actions and processes are part of the realm of micropolitics. (Blasé 1991, 11)*

Not all stakeholder groups have an interest in every decision being made, yet there are often competing needs and desires between and among the different groups. It is generally the principal's job to resolve these differences, to find areas of compromise and get things done. All stakeholder groups have the ability to wield their power and, in some cases, to unseat—or at least derail—the unwitting administrator.

Students

One would like to believe that, in schools, students are at the center of all decisions being made. Many mission statements include nifty phrases such as "every child counts" and "students come first," but, in the political arena, students do not have a lot of power. They do not set policy, allocate resources, or control the curriculum. They are mysteriously absent from the proverbial bargaining table. Their voices are not often heard among the cacophony of competing interest groups. When an administrator is considering which group has the most potential to create political problems or concrete rewards, students rarely make the list. One would like to believe that the school leader's personal values would keep the best interests of students in mind; however, this is not always the case.

Teachers

Teachers are the direct service providers hired to instruct all children. Teaching is an exhausting, complex, and rewarding endeavor—hundreds of decisions are made by the teacher each class period. There is a long tradition of autonomy within the classroom, and unwritten expectations held by teachers can make administrative imperatives, desires, and directives ineffective and politically challenging. As a group, teachers have become a powerful political constituency, able to influence administrative decisions at the site level. At the state level, unions and associations have become formidable political institutions that wield tremendous influence on educational policy.

Parents

Research often correlates the influence of parent involvement in a child's education and in the school system as a whole (Epstein 2001; Henderson and Berla 1994; Shaver and Walls 1998). With this constituency actively engaged in our schools, especially at the elementary level, it is no wonder that parents have demanded an increasing role in school governance and decision making. In the late 1990s, Chicago embraced major reform in which parents were granted a powerful role in overseeing local school administration (Bryk et al. 1999). Even without such direct institutional power, individual parents and special interest groups can exert tremendous influence on a site administrator's behavior and thinking. Not only do parents sit on committees with real decision-making authority—such as a school site council or a Parent-Teacher Association (PTA) that raises considerable sums of money—but in some school communities, parents understand that a simple phone call to a district office administrator or a school board member can have a significant influence on administrative decision making.

Community Members

Today, more than ever before, school leaders are soliciting the support of local businesses and community-based organizations to improve their schools. Rotary clubs, local universities, churches, city government, nonprofit organizations, and involved citizens can form strong partnerships with school leaders. In the best cases, these organizations offer time, energy, and financial resources to support local schools; in other cases, they attempt to extend their influence into the office of the principal as well as the classroom. Citizen action groups can prevent the construction of a "ball wall" at a middle school (because of concerns about noise on weekends), or they can provide meaningful mentorships or funding for music, arts, and athletics.

Upper-Level Administrators

This constituency includes superintendents, curriculum directors, personnel directors, fiscal directors, and school board members. All have influence on district policy and procedure, and, therefore, have institutional power and oversight of schools within the district. These individuals often are thought of as the "bosses" of the site-level administrators; thus, school leaders may be responsible for executing the will or whim of the upper-level administrators (not unlike middle managers). With all of these stakeholders peering down from above, decision making is rarely easy or lacking in scrutiny. Upper-level administrators may expect a school leader to control or influence teacher groups when politically charged differences surface; at the same time, school leaders must maintain positive and productive relations with the teachers and support staff with whom they work every day. Upper-level administrators can demand operational and instructional deliverables and create very challenging working conditions for the school leader.

Family

Although the family members of school leaders rarely are thought of as a stakeholder group in formal organizational theory, personal relationships can and do enter the field of administrative decision making. There are times when life outside the school setting—in the form of spouses, children, friends, and relatives—requires more than the usual amount of time and attention. It is not unreasonable to assume that a school leader may avoid certain decisions that will be overly time consuming or stress inducing. Many school leaders express a sense of being overwhelmed and may resent how consuming the position is, as well as how the relentlessness of the position negatively impacts their family life.

EXPLICATION OF INSTITUTIONAL
DECISION-MAKING INFLUENCES

It is not only individuals and stakeholder groups that inhabit the field of the school leader. Nonhuman factors also influence site administrators. Institutional expectations, fiscal concerns, state and federal goals and mandates, school reform efforts, academic research, and, finally, guiding principles—the personal values that come into play in the decision-making process—are examples of such influences. Following is an overview of the various stakeholders and constituencies, as well as nonhuman influences in the field, with which the school leader must negotiate.

Role Expectations

Although most positions in an organization include clearly elucidated job descriptions, the unwritten norms, expectations, and pressures for an employee to behave in a certain way are of equal importance. The "logic of appropriateness" (March and Olsen 1984) describes the institutional pressures to conform to these unwritten paradigms and beliefs. Role expectations are the net result of the conflicting and ongoing pressures exerted by students, teachers, parents, community members, and upper-level administrators. Role expectations and social pressures serve to constrain administrative choice and provide a "safe harbor" for decision making. Such institutional pressures may ensure the consistency and stability of our educational institutions, but they also can make deviations from the status quo quite difficult for the school leader.

Fiscal Concerns

Money is one kind of power, and the site-level administrator is responsible for overseeing and managing a variety of budgets, including general program funding, categorical program budgets (Title I, English language learner, drug and tobacco education, gifted and talented, textbook and library, school improvement, etc.), student body funds, community foundation monies, and parent association budgets. Each of these pots of money brings with it a different set of legal requirements, institutional expectations, and stakeholder desires, and the process of spending these monies can involve or disenfranchise different stakeholder groups. Each budget represents opportunity, responsibility, and a tremendous pressure on the school leader. Because there is very little financial slack in school organizations, the ability to offer monies to different groups or projects is regularly scrutinized, coveted, and complained about by different stakeholders in the school community.

District, State, and Federal Goals

District, state, and federal policy makers are charged with crafting a vision and setting policy. They often set ambitious goals, implement a system of rewards and punishments, or issue legal mandates to influence the ways in which educators behave. Labaree (1997) argues that the central problem of our educational system is the political struggle over the goals of education. Without specific rewards and punishments, general goals and objectives issued from the state and federal government (such as Goals 2000) will have little impact on administrative decision making. When there are no specific consequences for making progress in a particular area, a school leader is not likely to pay attention to it. On the other hand, when the state offers financial rewards to individuals, sites, and school districts (for example, when the state of California offered individual and site-level rewards for an increase in the Academic Performance Index, which is based on the California standards test), school leaders may be more inclined to shift priorities, resources, and areas of attention.

School Reform Efforts

In "Reforming Again and Again and Again," Larry Cuban (1990) identifies three primary, recurring reforms that swing like a pendulum through our educational environment. Classroom pedagogical reforms represent a battle between teacher-centered (didactic) instruction and student-centered (constructivist) instruction. Curricular reforms swing from the academic to the practical. While the academic reformers push for a rigorous college preparatory curriculum for all students, the practical reformers argue that students should be allowed to choose areas of study according to their interests, abilities, and future employment. A third area of reform concerns authority, specifically centralized versus decentralized control. Decentralized reformers assume that locals know best, and local control is seen as the embodiment of a responsive, democratic ideal. The centralized reformers believe in one best system, whereby the state—or even the federal government—sets standards, curriculum, and assessments that all local school districts are expected to implement. The school reform preferences dictated by policy makers, politicians, and upper-level administrators will define the systems and structures within which the school leader must operate, even if such reforms rarely are enforced at the local level.

Research

School leaders of today should at least be aware of, if not influenced by, current educational research. Articles and books (especially this one!) have the ability to impact a school leader's thinking and conceptualization of his or her practice. But such influence can occur only *if* a school leader recognizes the value and makes the time to engage with a research-based text (time is a very precious commodity to the school leader). Unfortunately, a tremendous disconnect often exists between theoretical scholarly writings and the practitioners who might benefit from such academic research.

Personal Values/Guiding Principles

All human beings have passions and preferences as well as personal nonnegotiables—words or behaviors that will not be tolerated. At the same time, those behaviors and practices that are highly valued by school leaders will be supported and promoted. Guiding principles can manifest as a push for social responsibility and community service or the promotion of a love for reading and literature. Guiding principles also influence which roles school leaders choose to play and how they choose to play them.

A COMPENDIUM OF DECISION-MAKING INFLUENCES

Figure 6.1 is a graphical representation of the field in which school administrators must operate, including the constituencies that vie for attention. Each influence represents a different but connected set of dangers, pitfalls, and, of course, opportunities.

The heuristic in Figure 6.1 shows the pressures that continually work on school leaders—pulling, pushing, and twisting them in many different ways. But what prompts a school leader to move in one direction or another, to favor one individual or stakeholder group over another? Wilson explains the consideration and impact of various influences on the school leader:

> *When bureaucrats are free to choose a course of action, their choices will reflect the full array of incentives and threats operating on them: some decisions will reflect the need to manage a workload; others will reflect the expectations of workplace peers and professional colleagues elsewhere; still others may reflect their own convictions. (1989, 66)*

Figure 6.1

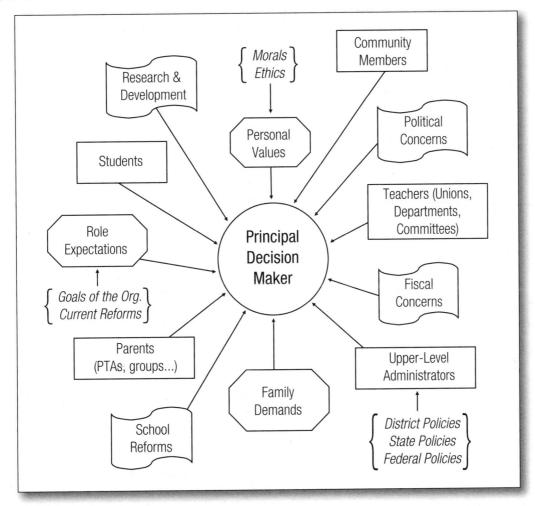

Value conflicts have become the norm in school systems. Both the internal and external environments add pressure to the role of the school leader. Indeed, the world of the school leader is a place filled not only with books and blackboards, but also with carrots and sticks.

A TOOL FOR EXPLICATING UNDERLYING INFLUENCES AND VALUES

The narratives captured from new school leaders engaged in reflective storytelling offer a peek into their thought processes, their guiding principles, and their emotions as they make difficult decisions. Whenever a school leader weighs the different choices available, considers the influence of different stakeholders, or measures the possible consequences of any given decision, that decision maker is engaging in the art and science of *values voting*. The underlying considerations that prompt a principal decision maker to act will reflect what is most meaningful and important to that individual and organization. Etzioni (2001) argues that decision making is a process of values clarification and that the prioritization of personal values is not so difficult. He claims that most individuals within an organization are readily able to rank their goals and priorities.

The following narratives present instances in which school leaders pull back the curtain and reveal some of the influences on their decisions and actions. These stories often are filled with rich descriptions of the intense emotion with which the school leader must contend, signaling that an overt or internal struggle is taking place.

TRUTH OVER HARMONY

Charles B. (October 2003) is an assistant principal at a high school who was working to bring about a systemic change at the site level. Although Charles did not initiate the development of small learning communities, he was firmly on board with this initiative. Unsurprisingly, there was dissent among some of the teachers; change can be quite difficult for many individuals. One of the senior teachers, a personal friend of the principal's, was putting up roadblocks to derail the reform effort.

> *It turns out the teacher pulled something over on the principal or was working stuff behind the scenes. [She told the principal], "All the teachers are really going to have a problem with this. They're all talking about it." It turns out that it's just her and her friends who are talking about it, but she's telling the principal that everybody's against the reform.*

Charles decided to work with the principal to address the situation, and he had the principal set up a meeting with the recalcitrant teacher. This is significant because Charles innately understood that, for this initiative to be fully implemented, the principal needed to be on board. In his story, Charles noted the challenges he faced, including the fact that the teacher was thirty years his senior:

> *I asked her if she was really on board with the restructuring process or whether she was actively working against it. She started crying.*

Charles is clearly not a leader who messes around. He got right to the heart of the matter, and such a bold question resulted in a strong emotional response. In education, it is not unusual for new school leaders to dance around an issue rather than putting concerns directly on the table for discussion and review. Although Charles knew that the principal had a long-standing relationship with the teacher, he was comfortable with his own professional relations with his boss and acknowledged, "The principal and I work well together." But the conversation with the teacher continued in its emotional intensity:

> *I would get a little overwhelmed by some of the aggressiveness or her questions or her defensiveness to my questions… I was forced to play the confrontational role in calling her on things. In the end, she implied that she may not come [to the professional development meeting] tomorrow, or, if she does come, she's just going to sit quietly and not say anything.*

This was definitely a victory for Charles. Quiet acquiescence can be preferable to direct opposition or behind-the-scenes undermining. During the questioning phase of the storytelling process, Charles was commended for taking such a big risk, but be felt that the conditions in the school enabled him to make the necessary decisions based on his personal guiding principles. He also demonstrated deep reflection and big-picture thinking as he framed his participation in the change process:

> *Because of the school that I'm at, I'm able to listen and fantasize about ideals. You can actually strive toward some ideals. I know there's no way that this group will come together as a collaborative group without addressing these issues… One of the foundations of a small learning community is that you work in collaboration with teachers… That's a big threat to some teachers.*

Charles was willing to take risks to further his vision of the ways in which this large, urban high school should be organized. He talked about the school community providing an opportunity for him to "strive toward some ideals." Although Charles was not explicit about what ideals he was striving for, he obviously valued "collaboration," and he did not describe any actions taken for his own self-interest. Charles readily accepted the political risks when he chose to play a "confrontational role" with a teacher who was good friends with the principal. Charles shared his recognition that personal loyalties might be of greater importance to the principal than the ideal aspirations of a school reform effort. By the mere fact that the principal was not assertive in addressing the resistant behavior, we can presume that the principal's passion probably does not match Charles's for building professional learning communities. The confrontation with the resistant teacher could have jeopardized Charles's relationship with not only the principal, but also a segment of the teacher population. Nonetheless, Charles continued moving toward his desired outcome.

After I read through Charles's narrative, I rated my perception of the influences exerted on Charles using a *Decision-Making Influence Matrix* (Figure 6.2) that lists the most common influences on the school leader. Using this tool can illuminate the specific areas of concern for Charles. This prioritization might be meaningful to Charles if he were to complete the matrix himself and use it as part of his own process of self-reflection.

Charles's decision to work alongside the principal to confront the oppositional (and dishonest) teacher was an expression of his personal values, his desire for honesty, and direct communication. His effort to promote teacher collaboration as a means to improve student learning (assuming that this was the reason for the restructuring) took precedence over ignoring or acquiescing to the desires of an individual teacher or the complacent principal. It is interesting to note that students were never directly mentioned in Charles's narrative; however, the reform itself appears to represent their interests more than any other constituency.

Figure 6.2 *Charles's Decision-Making Influence Matrix*

	High Concern	Some Concern	Little Concern	No Concern
Personal Values	❧			
Community Members	❧			
Political Concerns			❧	
Teacher Groups		❧		
Fiscal Concerns				❧
Upper-Level Administrators			❧	
Dist., State, and Federal Policies				❧
Family/Personal Demands				❧
School Reforms	❧			
Parent Groups				❧
Role Expectations		❧		
Student Groups	❧			
Research		❧		

In this narrative, Charles valued truth over harmony. He was willing to put himself in an uncomfortable position to ensure that the truth about how individuals behave behind the scenes came to light. He was not afraid to challenge others, regardless of their alliances. Charles stated very clearly that ideals are worth pursuing—even if feathers are ruffled in the process. One can bet that the interaction between Charles and the teacher was brought up in the faculty room and that there was, no doubt, a ripple effect throughout the larger teacher community. But Charles never expressed concern about the political ramifications of his decision.

AUTHENTICITY OVER OUTCOMES

In another narrative that depicts decisions being made based on strong personal convictions, Gretchen C. (November 2002)—an assistant principal at a high school—shared a story that had a profound impact on her professional practice:

> *I'll give you the end of the story first: I've just filed my first-ever complaint to the district against a parent on the basis of sexual harassment having to do with my sexual orientation. So, it's pretty deep.*

Gretchen told the story of a parent accusing her of "manhandling" the parent's child. When Gretchen met with the parent, she admitted to physically turning the female student around and speaking in a very stern voice. But, in Gretchen's narrative, the parent repeatedly cut Gretchen off when she tried to tell her side of the story. Gretchen was being polite and "Ma'am-ing her to death."

> *I started to say something, and she said, "My name is not Ma'am. My name is blah blah blah. What's your name? Billy? Bob? Pat?" At which point I was, like, coming out of my chair… She's really angry at me. And I'm still assuming it's over this incident. And when she did the "Billy, Bob, Pat," I'm like, oh. Oh, I see where we're going on this. This is a gay thing. Okay.*

This was a very disconcerting interaction for Gretchen. Although she did not take any action immediately after the exchange, she described another scene that took place a couple of weeks later, when Gretchen took her own mother on a tour of the school. The same parent made homophobic comments, accusing Gretchen of introducing "her lover" to the students in the school. This added fuel to the fire and prompted Gretchen to file a sexual harassment complaint. During the reflective storytelling process, one colleague posed a poignant question:

Questioner: *What is your expectation of what the district will do? Just call the parent and let her know?*

Gretchen: ***I don't know. I don't know. Let them figure that out! I just want it documented.***

Questioner: *Can I ask a question? How do you separate your personal from your professional life?*

Gretchen: ***I mean, it's hard for me because I really do think that my sexual orientation has to do with who I am as a person, and that's a personal belief… I could totally put up a picture of me and my brother and pretend that it's me and my husband—and lead this totally closeted life to my students. But, I can't. I could do that, but I can't. Either way, it takes a personal toll.***

This is a very important interaction because it elucidates several implicit and explicit decisions that Gretchen made. First, it is clear that Gretchen actively chose not to hide her sexual orientation. Although she understood that her openness might create problems for her, she was unwilling to play an inauthentic role. She struggled to find agency in her role as assistant principal without denying who she is as a person. Gretchen's second decision—to file a grievance—was a bit more perplexing, in that the act of filing a grievance requires intention, purpose, and action. Surprisingly, Gretchen was unable to identify her intended outcome. She stated that she wanted the harassment documented, but she didn't express a desire to have the parent stay off the campus, and she didn't consider other options in her narrative.

Gretchen obviously understood that her decision to file a grievance would inform a greater number of people at the district level about her sexual orientation and the fact that a parent was harassing her about this. This decision could have been a means of affirming her personal identity; it could have been a test to see how the district would respond to a politically challenging situation; or it could have been that Gretchen merely wanted emotional support and direction in dealing with a homophobic parent.

Interestingly, the initial problem described in the narrative was about Gretchen putting hands on a student when she was angry. The mother of the child was very upset about this incident and wanted Gretchen to reflect on the way she redirected her daughter. Yet, because of the parent's incendiary words, Gretchen's focus was directed almost exclusively toward the parent. Nowhere in the narrative did Gretchen reflect on her own behavior, or her interaction with the student.

By using the decision-making influence matrix (Figure 6.3), Gretchen's priorities can be revealed as she reflects on how she worked through this provocative situation. This process of analysis can be useful to novice administrators who may not be aware of the influences on their decision-making process. If Gretchen's personal values take precedence over factors and influences in the situation she is confronting, it may be helpful for her to see these priorities in a material form.

When a decision-making matrix is filled in based on words and actions described in Gretchen's story, it becomes apparent that her guiding principles were the primary, if not exclusive, influence on the way she handled the situation. Gretchen was clear that she had been wronged, and she felt compelled to take some kind of action. She exercised her right to file a grievance against the parent, and she expected that the district would follow through according to the written policy—even though she was not clear about the details. For Gretchen, the need to address sexual harassment superseded other institutional concerns or responsibilities. She explained, "[I could] lead this totally closeted life to my students. But, I can't. I could do that, but I can't." Gretchen must have known that, by filing a personal grievance, she risked having her own behavior—putting hands on students—come under greater scrutiny. She risked political and disciplinary action. Again, this was never mentioned in her narrative; therefore, one can only speculate that the political concerns and possible repercussions from higher-level administrators were not strong influences on her decision-making process.

Figure 6.3 *Gretchen's Decision-Making Influence Matrix*

	High Concern	*Some Concern*	*Little Concern*	*No Concern*
Personal Values	✺			
Community Members				✺
Political Concerns				✺
Teacher Groups				✺
Fiscal Concerns				✺
Upper-Level Administrators				✺
Dist., State, and Federal Policies		✺		
Family/Personal Demands				✺
School Reforms			✺	
Parent Groups				✺
Role Expectations				✺
Student Groups				✺
Research				✺

OUTCOMES AND AVOIDANCE

In another story that illuminates how a school leader's guiding principles can influence decisions, interactions, and actions, Maxine D. (October 2003)—a new assistant principal at an elementary school—described an unsettling situation. As a former special education teacher, one of the first things that Maxine noticed was that some of the special education aides served a very select and limited number of students. They were providing more support than was actually needed to some students, while other students with more serious needs were being underserved and sometimes ignored. Maxine was concerned about equity and the allocation of scarce resources, but—based on her past experience— she decided it was best to move cautiously to achieve her desired outcome:

> *I'd already gotten my toes a little bit stepped on. I don't think I was moving too fast, but anyway, there was this whole story I told last time about somebody going to the school board about me at a cocktail party. It was a small town… saying that I was moving things too fast… [What] I wanted to do was have the one-to-ones [paraprofessionals] start covering those other kids.*

As Maxine brought her colleagues up to speed, she shared her past experience and the corresponding political implications of moving too fast. Although this may not seem like a particularly challenging situation, Maxine explained that the paraprofessionals had been working with the same set of students for many years, and their behaviors and alliances with the students had become somewhat entrenched. Rather than take direct responsibility for changing the students of focus for the special education aides, Maxine looked for outside support:

> *The head of special ed. came to the district last year; he came at the superintendent's request. The superintendent loves him… I told [the special ed. director] that I think we could do the same thing… and use the paras we have to support these other kids, and he thought that was great. And I said, "I want you to do it. I'll sit in this meeting, I'll support you, but I want this idea to totally come from you." He was willing to do that.*

At this point, Maxine had determined what should get done and how it should happen. Although Maxine was able to effectively avoid confrontation with the special education staff, it is not surprising that her superiors raised some questions about her leadership and her willingness to address difficult situations:

> *He did go back to the superintendent and ask how come I was being so cautious. So when he asked me that later, I said, "If you can't figure that out… I've got to be. I'm new here and I don't have everybody's support yet." So we're in the process of making that happen, and I think it's going to work very well. It's much easier doing that than just me sitting down with the special [ed.] teacher and also the regular classroom teachers that were willing to move from having this one-to-one with the para… [I'm] learning to use other people in the school and in the district to fight my battles.*

It is interesting to note how comfortable Maxine was with having other people in the district handle her direct responsibilities. In this instance, Maxine was more concerned with meeting her objective and avoiding confrontation with her paraprofessionals than with how she might be perceived by her superiors. Notice her single-minded focus on working with this group of stakeholders in her school community.

And I'm just happy it worked. I don't care so much that… well, I do care that I'm not making enemies along the way. I'm learning the politics of dealing with it, and I think that's very important. I'm glad I'm coming out of this alive.

In this particular passage, Maxine described her willingness to have the special education director take a stand rather than face the probable resistance from the special education staff herself. At the end of the day, she was able to successfully implement the desired policy change and more equitably serve the students in the program. However, while Maxine claimed to be "learning the politics of dealing with it," she seems to have missed the political implications of redirecting her power and decision-making authority to upper-level administrators. The decision-making influence matrix in Figure 6.4 clearly shows Maxine's priorities.

Figure 6.4 *Maxine's Decision-Making Influence Matrix*

	High Concern	Some Concern	Little Concern	No Concern
Personal Values	✸			
Community Members				✸
Political Concerns		✸		
Teacher Groups	✸			
Fiscal Concerns				✸
Upper-Level Administrators				✸
Dist., State, and Federal Policies			✸	
Family/Personal Demands				✸
School Reforms		✸		
Parent Groups				✸
Role Expectations				✸
Student Groups	✸			
Research				✸

Maxine had a greater number of influences in her decision-making process than Gretchen did, but her primary interests—expanded service for special education students and avoidance of conflict at the site level—overshadowed her considerations of how her decision might be perceived by higher-level administrators.

The reflective storytelling process and the Decision-Making Influence Matrix are tools that can be used to expose the underlying values and priorities of school leaders. The matrix can provide an easy way for school leaders to analyze their narratives and better understand the influences that shape their decisions. Indeed, when school leaders see their priorities and underlying values expressed in the form of a material artifact, the results can be rather startling, discomforting, and angst inducing. Nonetheless, as Badaracco asserts, the process of self-reflection is imperative:

> *[When school leaders are able to] take time out from the managerial tasks that consume their time and undertake a process of probing self-inquiry—a process that is more often carried out on the run rather than in quiet seclusion—they are able to dig below the busy surface of their daily lives and refocus their core values and principles. (1998, 91)*

It is frightening to consider that some school leaders never take the time to reflect on their practice—they operate without clarity regarding who they are or what they stand for. C. S. Lewis (1974) described the danger of serving without a clear set of values when he wrote: "Education without values, as useful as it is, seems rather to make man a more clever devil." Indeed, schools are conflict-ridden places, and situations that hold the greatest amount of tension can boil and roil the emotions of the reflective school leader. However, it is important to note that all is not conflict filled in the world of education. Narratives about doing noon-duty supervision, counting the minutes for each schedule to accommodate a student council election assembly, or writing the weekly newsletter are not particularly story worthy. These managerial functions are important to the efficient operations of a school; however, they do not effectively describe the more meaningful and relevant decisions and actions of a school leader. It is in the areas of conflict and tension that school leaders are able to show who they are and what they stand for.

Champy (1995, 78) argues that "Values are the link between emotion and behavior, the connection between what we feel and what we do." He goes on to describe the uncertain, ever-changing environment in which school leaders are expected to operate. Values, he ascertains, can and should serve as "moral navigational devices." The field in which a school leader operates is very complex: it is inhabited by a variety of stakeholders, conflicting expectations, and influences. With every role that is played, and with every decision that is made, priorities and values are expressed. As Ralph Waldo Emerson neatly elucidated, "What you do speaks so loud that I cannot hear what you say."

Reflective Questions for Prospective and Practicing School Leaders

∞   What do you value most as a school leader?

∞   Do you regularly articulate your school's vision and values to the larger community? Is this important to do? Why?

∞   What type of language or behavior can you simply not accept? Why?

∞   What are some of the ways that you express your core values in the school setting?

∞   What are some of the actions you take that are misunderstood or misinterpreted by others? Why does this happen? What can be done to mitigate this situation?

∞   What personal values do you need to put aside or ignore in order to get along with others and be perceived as a successful school leader?

∞   How do your personal values and your corresponding roles and expectations as a school leader overlap? Do you have the authority to act on your beliefs and values?

∞   What do you do when your position demands that you act in ways that are incongruent with your personal values?

∞   How do you respond when individuals in the school community say that they will "agree to disagree" with you?

∞   What are the ways in which you seek to understand others? Why is this important?

Chapter 7

THE SCHOOL LEADER AS PRINCIPAL DECISION MAKER:
A Field of Dreams, Deliberations, and Derailments

Alice:	*Would you tell me, please, which way I ought to go from here?*
The Cat:	***That depends a good deal on where you want to get to.***
Alice:	*I don't much care where.*
The Cat:	***Then it doesn't much matter which way you go.***
Alice:	*...so long as I get somewhere.*
The Cat:	***Oh, you're sure to do that, if only you walk long enough.***

 Lewis Carroll, Alice in Wonderland, *1866*

Effective school leadership involves much more than knowing what roles you are expected to play and what you care about; it also involves setting a vision that has clear outcomes. One of the most common failures of school leaders is best described by Lewis Carroll: they know that they are supposed to be leading the organization, but they don't always know where they should be heading. The school leader must begin with the understanding of where one is (current state) and the vision of where one wants to be (goal state). Cognitive scientists, psychologists, linguists, philosophers, and sociologists offer unique perspectives regarding human thought, intuition, and the various approaches to leadership and decision making. However, the path from intentions to outcomes is not always clear or transparent. The art of leadership not only involves communicating the vision, it also involves charting a course, moving toward action, and motivating others to walk a particular path. Decision making is the engine of educational leadership.

When I use the term *principal decision maker* in this chapter, I am referring to those individuals—generally *principals*—who are granted the authority and responsibility to work with the students, staff, parents, and community and achieve the goals and objectives of the organization. This involves making decisions, big and small, to get the right things done. The word *principal* means "primary," as in the place where the proverbial buck stops. Although this book looks specifically at school leaders, the exploration of decision making can be applied to principal decision makers in any organization and any setting.

Decision making has been described as "a micro-political process which embraces a whole set of formal and informal areas of interaction, confrontation and negotiation," all of which are necessary to achieve a desired outcome (Ball 1987, 237). Most decisions of consequence require thoughtfulness, judgment, and the ability to read people and situations. Effective school leaders must remain engaged in a range of metacognitive processes. Each step in the decision-making process offers its own unique set of challenges and opportunities to make progress toward a particular goal or objective. Herbert Simon (1945) provides a basic framework for a rational decision-making process, but this is not necessarily how most school leaders are able to make decisions in the frantic world of site administration. He suggests

- listing alternative strategies;

- determining consequences of each; and

- comparing consequences *before* making a decision.

Although this is a good foundation for decision making, Simon left out some critical components. Before a problem can be solved, a situation calling for action must first be recognized. Every leader relies on a personal frame to gather information, make judgments, and frame the challenges that emerge in the field. Bolman and Deal (1997) describe the process of problem framing as using a lens to bring a particular issue into focus. Once an issue or area of concern has been identified as worthy of pursuit by the school leader, problem framing or agenda setting can also be used to put forward those issues that will be addressed by the organization by presenting them in a motivating, manageable, and palatable form.

School leaders also must formulate a clear decision-making process based on the particular challenge being faced. Thoughtful leaders must consider who will be involved in the decision making and how they will be involved. Principal decision makers must determine whether decisions will be made in isolation, with input from a committee, through consensus, or by a democratic process.

Once a school leader has identified a problem to be addressed and formulated a decision-making process, a form of *consequence analysis* follows (Schön 1983; Bolman and Deal 1997; Etzioni 2001; Hammond, Keeney, and Raiffa 2001). This component of decision making often begins with a review and analysis of the information and data available. In many school districts, school leaders have access to vast electronic data warehouses to store and retrieve relevant information; however, having access to information and data does not necessarily make the process of decision making any easier. Etzioni opines:

> If executives once imagined they could gather enough information to read the business environment like an open book, they have had to dim their hopes. The flow of information has swollen to such a flood that managers are in danger of drowning; extracting relevant data from the torrent is increasingly a daunting task. Little wonder that some beleaguered decision makers—even outside the White House—turn to astrologers and mediums. (2001, 46)

Consequence analysis is all about choosing the best available option based on the relevant and accessible information; it is a reflective activity that is sometimes used to avoid unintended or negative consequences. But when all is said and done, the actual practice of consequence analysis has not changed much since the days of Benjamin Franklin, who in 1772 described his process of decision making using a simple T-chart:

> ...writing over the one [column] Pro, and over the other Con. Then, during three or four days consideration, I put down over the heads short hints of the different motives, that at different times occur to me, for or against the measure. When I have thus got them all together in one view, I endeavor to estimate their respective weights... And though the weight cannot be taken with the precision of algebraic quantities... I have found great advantage from this kind of equation, in what may be called moral or prudential algebra. (Hammond, Keeney, and Raiffa 2001, 42, 43)

Another significant component of the decision-making process is the consideration of personal values, the guiding principles of the school leader. Chapter 6 discussed the ways that educators are confronted with a barrage of issues, challenges, and priorities, all of which beg for attention and the allocation of scarce resources. Ultimately, principal decision makers express their personal values and priorities through their decisions and actions. As many new administrators work to find agency in their new roles, some ask themselves, "Is this an issue I am able and willing to take on? Is this a mountain I am willing to climb?" Although not all challenges present dire consequences, valuing and prioritizing are integral components of the decision-making process.

A final step in decision making involves determining who is to be responsible for carrying out the actions, and how the implementation will be monitored. Drucker, a researcher on corporate decision making, explains, "The flaw in so many policy statements... is that they contain no action commitment—to carry them out is no one's specific work and responsibility" (2001, 13). It is not enough simply to make a decision. It is also imperative to define a clear action plan and to determine what actions will be taken, who will carry them out, and how the outcome will be measured as successful.

The relentlessness of the work faced by new administrators, the profound organizational demands, and the differing expectations from individuals and stakeholder groups can make thoughtful, analytical thinking quite difficult in the school setting. When discussing a *rational* decision-making process, Brett F. (January 2004)—a first-year middle school principal—became irritated as he explained:

> ❝ It is not as though I can leisurely sit at a desk, tape a large sheet of butcher paper on the wall, gather interested colleagues to brainstorm a long list of alternatives, and then, one by one, consider all possible outcomes for each alternative listed. No, no, no. In the time it takes to organize this process, four more e-mails will have made their way onto my computer, three students will have lined up awaiting appropriate discipline, two parents will have left messages, pissed off about one thing or another, and a teacher will be filing a formal grievance with the teachers' union about some other decision I made. ❞

So how does the overwhelmed administrator function with little time to engage in a rational decision-making process? Chester Barnard (1938), one of the seminal organizational theorists, describes a "zone of indifference," which, simply stated, is the collection of required tasks the worker is willing to accept as part of the position. This can be thought of as part of the original agreement accepted by the school leader when he or she took the position. School leaders generally understand that they will be expected to make difficult and sometimes unpopular decisions; however, when goals are vague, following established procedures (in other words, going by the book) can provide a guide to low-risk decision making (Wilson 1989).

Unfortunately, most situations that require action do not present an easy, mutually agreed-on course of action. Many challenges offer a choice of options whereby one group of stakeholders is certain to be upset. The principal decision maker often will make compromises, sometimes choosing between the lesser of two evils. Simon (1945) describes the concept of "satisficing," which is the process of finding a course of action that is acceptable, that is good enough, and that will satisfy the expectations of the position. Implicit in this concept is a blending of *satisfying* and *sacrificing*. Given the quantity of stakeholders with which a principal decision maker must contend, one can understand why "satisficing" might not be such an unreasonable practice. Mere survival can become a focus for the well-intended school leader. As Barnard explains, "the egotistical motives of self-preservation and of self-satisfaction [can be] dominating forces" for the school leader (1938, 139).

Some researchers have argued strongly about the role that intuition plays in decision making. They point to chess masters who are able to play dozens of games concurrently and make winning decisions in a matter of seconds. Barnard offers the best explanation for these "intuitive" abilities: "The sources of these non-logical processes lie in physiological conditions or factors… mostly impressed upon us unconsciously or without conscious effort on our part. They also consist of the mass of facts, patterns, concepts, techniques, abstractions, and generally what we call formal knowledge of beliefs" (1938, 302). In other words, school leaders who have been in the business of decision making for some period of time develop a level of expertise that allows them to analyze the field, determine the variables of significance, and quickly weigh their level of import in the situation at hand. This does not mean that expert leaders are able to read the future. Rather, experienced leaders are able to call upon past experiences to recognize themes and patterns that may shed light on the ramifications for and reactions from various stakeholders within the school community. There is nothing intuitive about this process at all.

Researchers who study decision making (Leithwood and Steinbach 1995; Daley 1999; Argyris 1982; Hatano and Oura 2003) assert that expert school leaders display a greater level of awareness of the processes they are using when they make decisions. They are able to articulate clearly what influences their decision-making process, and what steps they intend to take prior to making difficult decisions. They are able to describe their use of information as well as their process of consequence analysis. Additionally, effective school leaders spend more time planning strategies and are more aware of the social contexts; they consider the likely reactions of various stakeholders in the school community. In sum, expert school leaders continually regulate their own problem-solving processes and actively engage in metacognitive practices as they make difficult decisions.

Influenced by the literature on expert decision making, I designed a Metacognitive Decision-Making Process Rubric (Figure 7.1) that allows researchers and practitioners to assess the ways in which decision-making components (awareness of challenge, awareness of guiding principle, awareness of institutional expectations, involvement of stakeholders, clarity of desired outcome, and clarity of decision-making process) are expressed in the stories that new leaders tell: (1) no description; (2)

some description, implied; and (3) clear, explicit description. It is important to note that even though principal decision makers may engage in metacognitive processes, they may not necessarily articulate them when they tell a story to colleagues. Nonetheless, by analyzing the various components described in the administrative narratives, one can begin to draw some conclusions about which components are regularly considered and which components are sometimes neglected.

Figure 7.1 *Metacognitive Decision-Making Process Rubric*

	No Description	*Some Description; Implied*	*Clear, Explicit Description*
Awareness of Challenge	Does not mention challenge at all.	Some description of challenge. Some framing of the issue calling for action.	Clear description of underlying issues/concerns. Focus on analyzing and understanding problem.
Awareness of Guiding Principle	Does not mention or allude to a guiding principle or underlying personal value.	Some mention of personal principles or values that are underlying. Alludes to personal "conscience."	Clear description of personal principles. Explanation of personal "non-negotiables."
Awareness of Institutional Expectations	Does not mention any role expectations or "mandates" from the institution.	Some mention of institutional expectations, things that "have to be done."	Explicit description of the positional responsibilities expected by the institution.
Consideration or Involvement of Stakeholders	Does not mention any involvement of stakeholders or express any consideration for their possible reaction.	Some mention of how others might perceive or be affected by the decision being considered.	Clear description of consideration and/or involvement of relevant stakeholders in the decision-making process.
Clarity of Desired Outcome	Does not mention intended outcome.	Some description of how they would like the situation resolved.	Clearly stated description of intended outcome.
Clarity of Decision-Making Process	Does not describe or imply any process of decision making.	Some mention of factors involved in the decision-making process.	Clear description of the way in which the problem will be approached. Step-by-step process is explicated.

STUDENT LEARNING AND INTERNAL ANGST

Brian S. (September 2004), a first-year high school assistant principal, began his narrative by summarizing a particular challenge he faced: a mother had asked Brian to gather the homework for her child who was out of school because he had committed an unnamed crime. The teachers and the guidance counselor didn't want to provide the student with the work that he had missed due to his suspension. They believed that, if the student failed his classes, it would be a "natural consequence" of his actions. In his narrative, Brian described how he was invested in providing an education for this student; he wrestled with the best way to "act as an advocate for the students" without building resentment among his teachers. Brian brought up the fact that the student was African American and in special education, implying that equity issues were being played out in this particular situation.

Brian's frustration mounted as he considered how to solve the problem, and he readily conveyed his discomfort in playing the role of principal decision maker. Notice the litany of questions that spill out during Brian's narrative:

> *What's the protocol here? Do I let him go? Do I let him die a quiet death? I don't know. I'm just going through my own dilemma, which is, "Do I go into some shark-infested waters that I don't know anything about? Do I wait and make a decision and delay? Or do I go in a totally different direction and just accept the fact that this person is not willing to cooperate with the kid? Why am I in this job? Why did I take on administration? Do I really doubt urban youth or am I a cheap salesman? What am I doing?" It's kind of really a question about ethics.*

This is quite a riff—an impressive series of questions that shows the kind of reflection and inquiry that can emerge when new leaders are given the opportunity to consider their challenges within the context of a professional learning community. Through the reflective storytelling process, Brian neatly described the basic components of his decision-making process, beginning with the problem framing of two overarching challenges: (1) how to effectively serve this student within a school culture that does not want to support certain students, and (2) how to comfortably and effectively inhabit his new administrative role.

Further clarifying his challenge, Brian began to tease out the conflicting institutional expectations: "Basically there's a philosophical argument going on amongst educators in this environment as to whether [the school setting] should be punitive or rehabilitative." As previously noted, the teachers and counselor took the punitive approach, and Brian positioned himself squarely in the rehabilitative camp. He expressed his guiding principles in no uncertain terms, and—because of the resistance he faced—he experienced intense emotion: "I'm seeing red. I believe my job is not only the nuts and bolts and the operations policy but to act as an advocate for the kids."

The questions that Brian posed in the beginning of his narrative show how he formulated an appropriate decision-making process internally. He began with the consideration of stakeholder involvement. Brian was committed to doing the right thing by first involving the key players: those who worked most closely with the student. When Brian failed to get the response he was looking for, when he realized that he was unlikely to achieve his desired outcome (keeping the student engaged in learning), he considered whose support he could solicit to help him out:

> *At this point I'm thinking, do I complain to the principal? Do I go to the superintendent?... The conclusion I came to was, you can't fight every single fight. And I thought that getting the parent back in the loop, and getting the parent to ask the guidance counselor and the RSP [resource specialist program] teacher, and frankly the rest of the teachers, might be a lot more effective than having a principal of the whole school call.*

Initially, it seemed as though Brian might give up on this particular situation, and on this student, when he arrived at the conclusion "you can't fight every single fight." But in the end, he made a decision to involve the parent—not to fight his battle, but because he believed this would help him to achieve his desired outcome. Brian described some of the roadblocks put up by other members of the community that he had to work through. Eventually, he achieved some success:

> *One of the comments [the teachers] made, which ticked me off, was they couldn't ask professionally of their colleagues to do extra work, which I thought was silly... In the end the kid got his lessons... At least two of his teachers brought him lessons, so the kid is essentially somewhat taken care of. So I sort of solved it.*

Although it appears the story had come to a satisfying conclusion, notice the number of qualifiers that Brian used in describing the outcome: "essentially," "somewhat," "sort of." Brian understood that the commitment to do whatever it took to support and educate the students did not run deep; there was much more work to be done with teachers and support staff. The metacognitive practices that Brian described in his story are highlighted in Figure 7.2.

As Brian's story continued, he reflected on the situation and considered how he might respond in the future. Labov and Waltetzky (1967) describe this part of the story as the *coda,* the portion of the story that returns the listener to the present:

> *It strikes me that there is... you know there is this minor, this one thing... a real attitude... And I'm wondering how hard I can fight effectively to make sure that these kids are taken care of. So that's why... philosophically I was really challenged. I felt that it really tested my grounding in a lot of ways. Am I going to stay with this advocacy course in the long run that I'm on? Or am I going to cave?*

Figure 7.2 *Brian's Metacognitive Decision-Making Process Rubric*

	No Description	*Some Description; Implied*	*Clear, Explicit Description*
Awareness of Challenge	Does not mention challenge at all.	Some description of challenge. Some framing of the issue calling for action.	*Clear description of underlying issues/concerns. Focus on analyzing and understanding problem.*
Awareness of Guiding Principle	Does not mention or allude to a guiding principle or underlying personal value.	Some mention of personal principles or values that are underlying. Alludes to personal "conscience."	*Clear description of personal principles. Explanation of personal "non-negotiables."*
Awareness of Institutional Expectations	Does not mention any role expectations or "mandates" from the institution.	*Some mention of institutional expectations, things that "have to be done."*	Explicit description of the positional responsibilities expected by the institution.
Consideration or Involvement of Stakeholders	Does not mention any involvement of stakeholders or express any consideration for their possible reaction.	Some mention of how others might perceive or be affected by the decision being considered.	*Clear description of consideration and/or involvement of relevant stakeholders in the decision-making process.*
Clarity of Desired Outcome	Does not mention intended outcome.	Some description of how they would like the situation resolved.	*Clearly stated description of intended outcome.*
Clarity of Decision-Making Process	Does not describe or imply any process of decision making.	*Some mention of factors involved in the decision-making process.*	Clear description of the way in which the problem will be approached. Step-by-step process is explicated.

Brian delved back into the story, analyzing and summarizing the challenge he faced. Storytelling is one way in which new administrators can make sense of and integrate new experiences. Notice the big-picture thinking that is taking place:

> *I felt like I was dealing with this calcified, kind of ossified system, and this guy who was out to punish the kid even worse than he'd been punished already. Not that the kid doesn't need to be locked up if in fact the kid has committed a crime, but this is apples and oranges. We're talking crime and punishment, education and work. It's seems to me to be apples and oranges—two totally different things. That wasn't too difficult a part of the dilemma. The part of the dilemma was how to fight.*

So Brian let the listeners know that, indeed, a battle had been waged and won; but the large war was still in progress. This is important from a practitioner's perspective because it shows that Brian is not done thinking about how this discrete situation fits into the larger context of his school community. Brian took his learnings from a particular situation and shared how he might apply them to similar situations that were likely to present themselves in the future. Brian was acquiring agency in, and ownership of, his role as a principal decision maker.

STUDENT RIGHTS VERSUS TEACHER SAFETY

Conflicts often result from the way that different stakeholders within the school community view a particular situation: students, teachers, parents, and administrators can see things very differently. These situations often require action, interventions, and difficult decisions from the school leader. Darlene D. (February 2003), a middle school assistant principal, described a challenge that showcased the conflicting perceptions and tensions that new administrators are expected to manage:

> *[I'm dealing with] an incident in our school where a sixth-grade, emotionally disturbed student pushed a teacher. The teacher happened to be eight months pregnant… I think that, yeah, we were in the wrong for not showing that teacher how to deal with him… [We are now considering if we will expel or allow him to come] back to our school. And in reality, we'd probably win at the hearing and let the expulsion go. But if we did, that just gives kids the idea they can push teachers. Not only that, the staff would lose control over the fact that we didn't do anything… [But] I have no qualms about [recommending him for expulsion], because the point is, he pushed a pregnant woman in the bushes.*

Just as Brian began his narrative with problem framing, so, too, did Darlene. Although Darlene claimed she had "no qualms" about expelling the student, one might ask why she felt compelled to tell this particular story. What became apparent in the beginning of her narrative was that Darlene did not have a clear guiding principle that informed her decision making; rather, she spent much of her story considering the perspectives of the different stakeholder groups. Her narrative portrayed the variables involved in the decision: to expel or not to expel. The institution required an expulsion—safety is of paramount importance, after all. In her decision-making process, Darlene thoughtfully considered how students and teachers might react and respond to her decision. She recognized that students needed to see that one of their peers could not "get away" with such a transgression, and the teachers needed to feel that their need for personal safety was being addressed.

When a special education student is being considered for expulsion, a manifestation determination must ensue (whereby the special education team determines if the transgression was a direct result of the learning disability). In this particular situation, one stakeholder group—the father of the child—had a clear idea about the appropriate course of action. Darlene shared her memory of the father's statement, in which he expressed his case very succinctly and powerfully:

> *What [my son] did was wrong, yes, but I don't think the school did anything to keep him from going down this route. I don't think the teacher handled the situation correctly. Really what I want is for my son not to get punished but for us to learn from what happened right now to, you know, for future children… for this not to occur, because there's obviously been something that got dropped here, that didn't occur correctly for my child to have success.*

Here, a clear chasm exists among stakeholder groups. Although Darlene initially was influenced more by the expectations of the institution, a shift occurred in her thinking when she began to reflect on the father's statement. Ultimately, she acknowledged the father's perspective, but she fretted about how the staff might respond if the student was not expelled:

> *[The school should have] taken care of its job of informing the teacher of how to deal with students who are emotionally disturbed and [ensure an understanding of] what will set them off. And in reality, we did in fact drop the ball… we're going to be in a very rough spot… There's no way they could let him back, not after what he did. And that's where I've been thinking about all the things we could have done differently. It's just strange.*

Although Darlene did not specifically describe the process she used to make her decisions and influence the outcome, it is clear that she was actively engaged in a process of consequence analysis. Still, Darlene did not clearly articulate a desired outcome. In addition, to reify the expression of personal angst, Darlene concluded her story by talking about the student: "And honestly, I like the kid; he's a very good kid… this kid's just bright."

Again, it is helpful to unpack Darlene's story and examine the metacognitive processes that she engaged in while working through this very challenging situation (see Figure 7.3).

During the process of reflective questioning, one of the other school leaders asked Darlene if she believed it was best for the child to return to the school. This question elicited a reframing of Darlene's perspective and enabled her to define a set of guiding principles—the importance of a fair and just learning environment for the student—that helped determine her decisions and actions. She answered the question with newfound conviction:

> *No! Not now, because the staff is going to be all over him. Everybody knows him. He would never get a fair shake from the staff now, never, especially because the staff is actually pretty tight.*

Figure 7.3 *Darlene's Metacognitive Decision-Making Process Rubric*

	No Description	*Some Description; Implied*	*Clear, Explicit Description*
Awareness of Challenge	Does not mention challenge at all.	Some description of challenge. Some framing of the issue calling for action.	*Clear description of underlying issues/concerns. Focus on analyzing and understanding problem.*
Awareness of Guiding Principle	*Does not mention or allude to a guiding principle or underlying personal value.*	Some mention of personal principles or values that are underlying. Alludes to personal "conscience."	Clear description of personal principles. Explanation of personal "non-negotiables."
Awareness of Institutional Expectations	Does not mention any role expectations or "mandates" from the institution.	Some mention of institutional expectations, things that "have to be done."	*Explicit description of the positional responsibilities expected by the institution.*
Consideration or Involvement of Stakeholders	Does not mention any involvement of stakeholders or express any consideration for their possible reaction.	Some mention of how others might perceive or be affected by the decision being considered.	*Clear description of consideration and/or involvement of relevant stakeholders in the decision-making process.*
Clarity of Desired Outcome	*Does not mention intended outcome.*	Some description of how they would like the situation resolved.	Clearly stated description of intended outcome.
Clarity of Decision-Making Process	Does not describe or imply any process of decision making.	*Some mention of factors involved in the decision-making process.*	Clear description of the way in which the problem will be approached. Step-by-step process is explicated.

So, by the end of her story, Darlene had acquired a clearer perspective of the situation and developed clarity regarding her core values. Although the legalities of the situation prevented the institution from expelling the student, Darlene concluded her narrative by describing the need to advocate for an alternative placement for the student, to protect the child. Through the reflective storytelling process, Darlene was able to settle on a new and more deliberate course of action.

SCHOOL RULES OR HUNGRY PARENTS

In another narrative that shows the decision-making challenges school leaders face, Steven G. (November 2003)—a second-year elementary school assistant principal—shared a detailed story that highlighted some of the personal angst he was working through. Steven was meeting with great resistance in his school community while attempting to fulfill what he perceived to be his role responsibilities. He was learning how difficult it could be to fulfill the institutional expectations:

> *We have 1,000 kids at our school… we probably get 100–110 kids to show up [for the free breakfast program]… The problem: parents were taking food out of the cafeteria, and then it becomes illegal and we could lose our program. Essentially, I had to go in and monitor the breakfast every day… We don't write the rules, we don't make legislation. We don't do anything. All we can do is get the rules handed to us and we are expected to implement them, and then in the meantime, make sure that everybody is happy. It sucks! I've pissed off just about everybody on the list: the parents, the students, the state—they've all got a piece of me.*

After explaining his responsibility to enforce the law and prevent parents from taking food that is part of the free breakfast program for children, Steven identified the strong emotion coming from the stakeholders in the school community. Parent expectations were unstated but very clear: they expected Steven to turn a blind eye to what happened in the cafeteria. As part of this reflective storytelling process, colleagues asked probing questions to get Steven to reflect on his intent, motivation, and desired outcome. Even when Steven was questioned forcefully by other participants during the reflective storytelling process, he stood by his decision to enforce the rule of law.

Questioner: *Do you feel like you're going to be audited by food services?*

Steven: ***No, but then again, that's when you're going to get audited.***

Questioner: *Are there any laws or regulations that are worth breaking?*

Steven: ***Oh yeah.***

Questioner: *So you don't feel like this is one?*

Steven: ***No. Is it part of my job? Am I going to do it because it's the law? Yes. Do I think it's right? No, I don't.***

In this case, Steven acknowledged that he did not believe that the law was right, but he was willing to enforce the law because of the possible consequences (to him or the school) that could come from outside the system. However, Steven remained cognizant of the stakeholder expectations within the community. He was uncomfortable and felt like he had upset most individuals and groups within his school community.

Yet, not everyone in his school was against him. During the storytelling process, Steven described the food servers' ongoing frustration with parents taking food from the cafeteria that was intended for the students. They had been angry that no administrator was willing to take on this issue, and they expressed appreciation that the new administrator addressed their concerns.

Steven also expressed fear that, if food services conducted an audit and found that food was being stolen, the entire free breakfast program could be jeopardized; those children for whom the program was created would be the ones to suffer because of the administration's complicity in parental stealing. One might wonder how realistic his concerns were, but Steven expressed this as a real fear and, in some districts, there are indeed norms and edicts that are fiercely enforced. On the other hand, this may be a rationalization—a justification invented after the decision was made—as described in the *garbage can model* of decision making. Cohen, March, and Olsen (1972) assert that "an organization is a collection of choices looking for problems, issues and feelings looking for decision situations… and decision makers looking for work." This theory suggests that the principal decision maker will plausibly and logically justify or explain a course of action after a decision has been made. In this specific narrative, it is also possible that Steven was genuinely motivated by the fact that stealing is wrong; as the administrator in charge, he had the responsibility to ensure that these moral transgressions did not occur under his watch.

In completing the metacognitive decision-making rubric for this example (Figure 7.4), the influences and processes that moved Steven to make decisions and take corresponding actions are clarified.

As a school leader and a representative of the institution, Steven communicated through his actions that upholding law and order was of higher value than allowing families to take food from the school cafeteria. This was not a subsidy Steven was willing to offer, a behavior he was willing to tolerate, or a risk he was willing to incur. If administration is the art of getting things done, of particular importance is *what* things get done and, for the reflective school leader, *why* things get done. It would be very interesting to have Steven color his own rubric, articulate how he made his decisions, and then describe the values that he expressed through his actions.

Figure 7.4 *Steven's Metacognitive Decision-Making Process Rubric*

	No Description	*Some Description; Implied*	*Clear, Explicit Description*
Awareness of Challenge	Does not mention challenge at all.	Some description of challenge. Some framing of the issue calling for action.	***Clear description of underlying issues/concerns. Focus on analyzing and understanding problem.***
Awareness of Guiding Principle	***Does not mention or allude to a guiding principle or underlying personal value.***	Some mention of personal principles or values that are underlying. Alludes to personal "conscience."	Clear description of personal principles. Explanation of personal "non-negotiables."
Awareness of Institutional Expectations	Does not mention any role expectations or "mandates" from the institution.	Some mention of institutional expectations, things that "have to be done."	***Explicit description of the positional responsibilities expected by the institution.***
Consideration or Involvement of Stakeholders	Does not mention any involvement of stakeholders or express any consideration for their possible reaction.	***Some mention of how others might perceive or be affected by the decision being considered.***	Clear description of consideration and/or involvement of relevant stakeholders in the decision-making process.
Clarity of Desired Outcome	Does not mention intended outcome.	Some description of how they would like the situation resolved.	***Clearly stated description of intended outcome.***
Clarity of Decision-Making Process	Does not describe or imply any process of decision making.	***Some mention of factors involved in the decision-making process.***	Clear description of the way in which the problem will be approached. Step-by-step process is explicated.

DECISION MAKING AND FEELINGS OF EFFICACY

In reviewing the literature on expert decision making and analyzing the administrative narratives, it becomes plain that two convergent but distinct processes take place when new leaders make difficult decisions. First are the internal considerations: the valuing, strategizing, and planning that generally take place prior to the public decision-making process. Also present is the external process of decision making that tends to appear more publicly and often is presented as thoughtful, deliberate, and more "superhero-like." Effective leaders do not allow important decisions to be made without their direct (though often covert) influence or without structuring the process to increase the likelihood that their desired outcome will be achieved. This means that Herbert Simon (1945) got it wrong when he described the rational decision-making process as listing alternative strategies, determining the consequences of each, and comparing the consequences *before* making a decision. Instead, the metacognitive skills involved—the reflective thinking, the clarity of the desired outcome, the awareness of one's guiding principle, the consideration and involvement of stakeholders—can be the more powerful components of the decision-making process. These processes generally occur away from the public eye.

Is this a form of manipulation and control or subversive activity? Strong leaders ensure that important decisions are made with their direct and indirect influence, and they have a vested interest in the outcome. They generally will be held responsible for the decisions being made, which is why it is so crucial for them to secure broad-based involvement and support in the decision-making process.

When looking at the set of administrative narratives and assessing whether the storytellers described a clear decision-making process to address the problem at hand, I was not at all surprised that only 107 of our narratives (43 percent) depicted school leaders who were clear, or somewhat clear, in the descriptions of their decision-making processes. These were, after all, primarily novice school leaders, and they were engaged in a process in which they shared "trouble stories" as a means of improving their practice. This does not mean that the school leaders were not making decisions and taking actions. Rather, it means that, in many situations, actions were being taken without a clear intended outcome—without a clear process of decision making.

In yet another pass through the narratives, I assessed overall feelings of efficacy in new school leaders. This is not to be confused with actual effectiveness in achieving desired outcomes. Rather, I appraised their feelings of competence as they made difficult decisions under challenging circumstances. In most of the narratives, school leaders expressed frustration and ineffectiveness in solving the problem that they were attempting to address. Feelings of efficacy were clearly low in 90 narratives (37 percent), and they were either neutral or unidentifiable in another 105 narratives (41 percent). Ultimately, there were 51 narratives (20 percent) in which the school leader expressed confidence and positive feelings of efficacy in working through a particular challenge.

Although I did not set out to find correlations between feelings of efficacy and clarity of decision making, when I sorted this data in a spreadsheet, I found that high feelings of efficacy were *always* accompanied by great clarity in the decision-making process. Of course, there were many narratives in which school leaders had a clear decision-making process but did not possess positive feelings of efficacy. But, given the transient and temporary tenure of most school leaders, it would seem that clear processes and protocols that engender positive feelings of efficacy might be an important lesson for school leaders who are interested in becoming more positive, effective, and contented—if they are to last in the profession. DuFour and Eaker explain:

If schools are to improve, they need educators who believe in the possibility of a better future—and in themselves. The link between success and self-efficacy—the belief that one has mastery over one's life and can meet challenges as they come up—has been well established. (1998, 285–286)

A METACOGNITIVE DECISION-MAKING FLOWCHART

After reviewing the literature on decision making and analyzing the leadership narratives, I created a Metacognitive Decision-Making Flowchart (Figure 7.5) that can help novice administrators avoid common pitfalls in problem-solving and ensure that all of the components of the decision-making process are at least considered. This flowchart differs from the typical decision-making heuristics in that it exposes the hidden thought processes—the metacognitive practices—that, when made explicit, can prevent some of the missteps that may lead to anger and frustration.

In the first stage of the metacognitive decision-making process, the school leader must identify a problem and deem it worthy of intervention. The underlying metacognitive processes include a preliminary review of the data at hand (which could include anything from low attendance to poor test scores, filthy bathrooms, raging parents, confrontational teachers, injured children, and so on). Additional reflective processes would also include a consideration of competing expectations, problems, concerns, and responsibilities that must be addressed. In other words, school leaders must determine their bandwidth and capacity, as well as the time, energy, and resources available to take on this newly recognized challenge. The end of step one overlaps directly with step two in raising the question, "Should this particular challenge become a priority?" School leaders examine their guiding principles and determine why the issue might be personally important, and why the issue might be important to various stakeholders and to the organization itself.

If the challenge rises to the level of importance at which school leaders are motivated to take some kind of action, it is imperative that these leaders develop clarity with regard to their intended outcome. It is shocking that so many stories are told in which actions are taken without any clear description of desired outcomes. Brett F. (May 2004), a middle school principal, shared a story in which he gave a hardworking secretary a poor evaluation because she was slow to complete the typing and paperwork that she was assigned. The story concluded with Brett's secretary quitting because she was so devastated by the evaluation. One of Brett's colleagues asked him if the secretary was working to the best of her ability and then exhorted:

> *This is a clear case of asking "pigs to fly." When you ask a pig to fly, when you ask them to do something they can't do, then the pig gets angry and you get frustrated. You said in your story that she was great at answering phones and greeting the public, and that you didn't think she could do her paperwork better or faster. Then what was your intended outcome when you gave her a bad evaluation? Did you want her to quit? What did you expect? Was it possible that you could have restructured her job to capitalize on her strengths?*

Figure 7.5 *Metacognitive Decision-Making Flowchart*

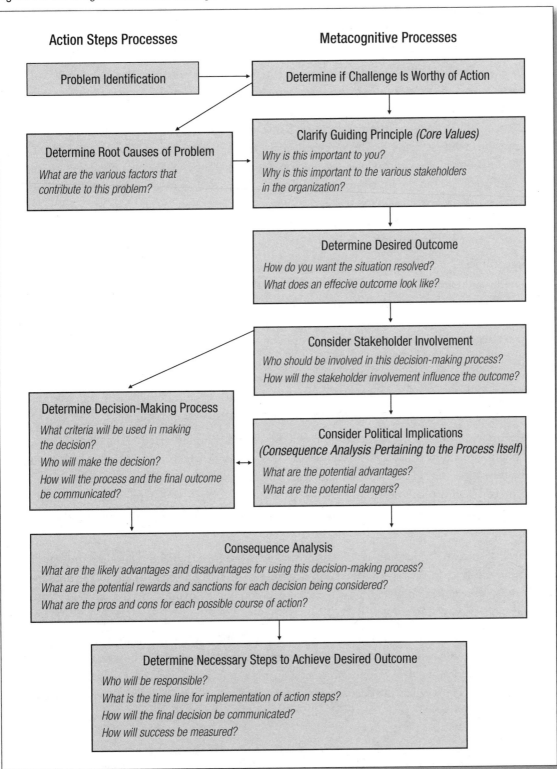

Brett explained that he was only thinking about his personal integrity and being honest rather than considering his intended outcome. Brett felt "sick to his stomach" and acknowledged that, if he could do it all over again, he would not have given her the evaluation as it was written. This brief story demonstrates the importance of determining a desired outcome very early in the decision-making process.

Once an intended outcome is clarified, the next stage in the metacogntive process can be undertaken: the consideration of which stakeholders to involve in the decision-making process. Even a school leader who cares about broad-based school/community involvement will not (and cannot) have all stakeholders involved in every decision. Some decisions are best left to small groups, while still other decisions are best made by the principal or the administrative team. For example, Rhonda C. (May 2005)—a high school principal—talked about teachers lobbying for the opportunity to teach at a particular grade level in the upcoming year. Rhonda made a deliberate decision to make the decision herself rather than have the teachers "tear each other apart. Better they should hate my guts rather than hate each other." The most important consideration in this particular stage is how involvement of an individual or stakeholder group will influence the intended outcome.

Next comes the transparent portion of the decision-making process: the determination or explanation of the process that will be used to make the decision. This stage in the process is highly political. Knowing that, when difficult decisions are made, disgruntled stakeholders will readily criticize the decision-making process that was used (as well as the way in which the final decision is communicated), the reflective practitioner needs to craft a thoughtful, detailed, transparent process for making a decision that includes consideration of the criteria used to make the decision, who will be involved in making the decision, how the actual decision will be made, and corresponding time lines. The metacognitive component involves a careful assessment of the potential risks and advantages in using the considered decision-making process before it is actually set into motion.

After a decision-making process has been established and communicated to the school community, a very public process of consequence analysis can take place, in which the pros and cons, advantages and disadvantages, and rewards and sanctions are considered, evaluated, and ultimately agreed upon. The irony is that this phase of the process—in which public input is generally sought—often is less important to determining a particular outcome than the hidden, metacognitive parts of the decision-making process.

The final stage of the decision-making process is all about management and follow-through. In this final (but critical) stage, the school leader will determine who will get the work done, the time frame in which the work will be completed, how the final decision will be communicated, and how success of the course of action will be measured.

The message for practitioners is very clear: the movement from novice to expert involves becoming more conscious, more deliberate, and more metacognitive in all phases of decision making. Admittedly, being reflective and thoughtful will not necessarily insulate a school leader from being the focal point of intense emotion. However, as the data suggest, school leaders can expect to *feel* more efficacious about their work as they become clearer about the decision-making process they are using.

Reflective Questions for Prospective and Practicing School Leaders

❧   What is an example of a decision you had to make that was difficult for you?

❧   Why was this decision challenging for you?

❧   Which kinds of challenges do you recognize and deem worthy of your time and energy? Why?

❧   How do you ensure that you fully and deeply understand the problem at hand? What is your process of root-cause analysis? What data points do you rely on?

❧   What are the consequences of ignoring or choosing not to get involved in particular issues or challenges?

❧   What are the micropolitics of the challenge(s) you wish to take on?

❧   Do you have the capacity (time, energy, resources, skill, and will) to address the challenges that you believe are most pressing? Why or why not?

❧   How can you draw on past experiences and learnings to strategically solve a challenge that calls for action?

❧   Who do you generally include in your decision-making processes when you face a particularly difficult challenge?

❧   What are the different decision-making bodies in your school community? What kinds of questions or issues do these different teams take on?

❧   Which dangers and which rewards are deemed most significant to you in the process of consequence analysis?

❧   What prompts you to do the things you do in your current position?

❧   Do you typically try to control the outcome when presenting decisions before a group or committee? Is this ethical?

❧   What would make you feel at ease, if not content, if you did not achieve your desired outcome after a difficult decision-making process?

Chapter 8

THE SCHOOL LEADER AS HUMAN PINCUSHION:
The Role of Emotions in School Leadership

Anyone can become angry—that is easy. But to be angry with the right person, to the right degree, at the right time, for the right purpose, and in the right way—this is not easy.

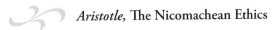

Aristotle, The Nicomachean Ethics

School leadership and strong emotion are inextricably intertwined; the challenges of working with and through intense emotion are prominent in almost every narrative that new leaders share. Clearly, there is a cathartic as well as an entertaining purpose in leadership storytelling: antagonists are frequently described as screaming or cussing, fussing and fuming, while protagonists often reveal their angst, frustration, and self-doubt. Many situations described by new school leaders include pleadings, political power plays, threats, and even acts of physical aggression. Frighteningly, 8 percent of the stories we heard included incidents of violence or threatened violence. It is no wonder that many new school leaders are uncomfortable in their new roles. Few new leaders are adequately trained to manage the turbulent situations and corresponding emotions that arise in the school setting. School leaders do not have superpowers—most merely aspire to serve as instructional leaders. Peter Reason explains:

Skills at working with emotional distress are not very widely available in our culture. We are more likely to close down, deny or otherwise defend ourselves against distressing feelings, than we are to bring them to awareness, work with them, abreact and understand them, and allow ourselves to move beyond them. It is therefore a clear advantage if an inquiry group has available to it a degree of optimal competence so that personal distress can be appropriately managed. (1988, 29)

Typical images of effective leaders include those who are cool under pressure, those who can calm troubled waters, and those who can navigate and redirect anger, frustration, and discontent. Roche (1999), in his study of how leaders respond to moral dilemmas and challenges, identifies the following as the most common responses: avoidance, suspended morality, creative insubordination, and, finally, taking a personal moral stance. According to Roche, avoidance is used most frequently; rarely do school leaders take a strong stand unless there is a high likelihood that they will achieve their desired outcome. These practices do not embody the qualities and actions of a superhero. Regardless of their approach or personal style, school leaders are expected to nimbly resolve challenging situations, ranting parents, angry students, disgruntled teachers, and irate neighbors; it does not matter what the rationale is for the intense emotions that accompany each challenge.

But why is so much intense emotion part of the stories that new administrators tell? What are the primary challenges and conflicts? What are the catalysts? How do new leaders cope with these emotions? In classic literary analysis, the most common struggles portrayed in stories are man versus man, man versus nature, man versus himself, and man versus society. When I investigated the administrative stories, I found that 39 percent of the narratives involved school leader versus individual teachers or teacher groups. This was a most unexpected finding, especially when compared with the total number of stories that described conflicts with students: 5 percent. These percentages are particularly significant given the fact that students typically outnumber teachers by a magnitude of twenty-five or more. Only 6 percent of the narratives described conflicts with parents or guardians, and 9 percent described conflicts with co-administrators or upper-level administrators. Figure 8.1 shows the number of conflicts with different stakeholders described in the stories, as well as internal conflicts and challenges with schoolwide systems and role expectations.

Figure 8.1

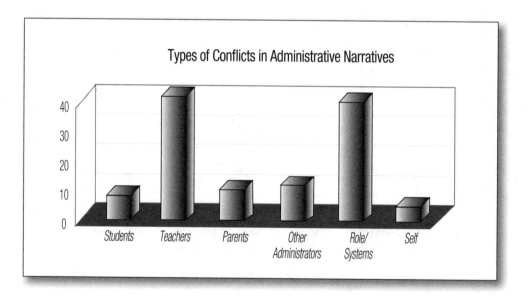

These data do not suggest that the majority of teachers are ineffective in their teaching, have negative attitudes, exhibit oppositional behavior, or regularly defy schoolwide norms and expectations. Rather, this graph merely represents the frequency of challenges described by new leaders in their narratives. One explanation for these findings is that a story about supporting teachers does not generate as much interest or possess the "tellability" that a story about protecting a child from a malicious teacher does. However, an analysis of narratives indicates that an ample number of teachers will require a significant amount of the school leader's time and energy to address inappropriate and unprofessional behavior. The work demands that school leaders have hard conversations, coach, evaluate, develop strategies of intervention, and provide progressive discipline. This part of the school leader's responsibilities requires vigilant thoughtfulness, planning, and emotional restraint.

Goleman, a foremost authority on *emotional intelligence*, describes the necessity of developing skills to marshal emotions when addressing challenging situations or individuals:

> *Much evidence testifies that people who are emotionally adept—who know and manage their own feelings well, and who read and deal with other people's feelings—are at an advantage in any domain of life, whether romance and intimate relationships or picking up the unspoken rules that govern success in organizational politics... people who cannot marshal some control over their emotional life fight inner battles that sabotage their ability for focused work and clear thought. (1995, 36)*

The bar is set very high for school leaders. While students, teachers, and parents are afforded great latitude in the way they express their feelings, this is not the case for the school leader. Even those leaders who appear to have mastered skills in emotional responsiveness express a deep frustration with the constraints of the role:

> 66 *The worst part about being a principal is I never get to use my sharp tongue. I've got to sit there and take it. I mean, I can destroy these people with my words... I have the ability to humiliate them, and I sit there and say, "I understand how you're feeling." (Brian F., October 2002)* 99

If school leaders are unable to control their emotions and they fail to develop skills in emotional intelligence, they will not last long in the profession. Although many new school leaders cite their ability to speak the truth and artfully engage in productive conflict, they often express difficulty in learning to cope with the intense emotion that they confront in their new role.

This is where reflective storytelling can be especially useful to novice school leaders. In moments of disequilibrium, describing uncomfortable situations in the form of a story can compel leaders to think critically about what got them into the mess in the first place. When new leaders take advantage of structured opportunities for reflection, they can deepen their understanding of the challenges they face, practice their metacognitive thinking, and reconsider their theories of action. Schön explains:

> *Reflection gives rise to on-the-spot experiment. But our reflection on our past reflection-in-action may indirectly shape our future action. The reflections of a Monday morning quarterback may be full of significance if the person reflecting is the quarterback who will play differently because of his Monday morning quarterbacking. (1987, 28)*

The following narratives provide examples of the common triggers to intense emotion and the ways new leaders navigate an ethical, political, and emotionally laden landscape.

AWARENESS OR LACK THEREOF

Max K. (December 2003), a second-year assistant principal at a large middle school, began his story by describing an information-gathering process that enabled him to identify a need in his school:

> *At the start of the school year I surveyed teachers individually and surveyed departments about what they felt their needs were or what they wanted out of professional development or personal support. The top two things were collaborative team lesson planning and peer observations.*

At first glance, setting up a program such as this does not seem to be a particularly Herculean challenge. However, Max was thoughtful about how best to proceed as he began a process of consequence analysis:

> *I didn't want to start this program and just throw teachers out there and say, "Okay, logistically it's set up. You observe this person at this time. You go into this teacher's classroom period on such a date and observe." I wanted us to have a real focus as a school... So I worked with a particular woman on the instructional leadership team to try to develop a focus for these observations and think... how can this help us out in our instruction? How can we help to prepare our faculty members for these periodic observations with this type of focus? A lot of the people on the leadership team were behind the idea.*

Max explained how this initiative addressed his desired outcome of creating an instructional focus at the school. However, Max was not making decisions independently. He talked about working with a woman on the leadership team to refine his focus and efforts. Although Max never explained how this team was formed or how it functioned, he clearly involved stakeholders and raised important questions to ensure a positive outcome. Max was interested in incorporating the team's ideas, but he also was compelled to provide a sharp focus to the peer observations. Notice the range of questions that Max presented:

> *They were also pretty enthusiastic about the fact that they wanted time to be able to observe for whatever it is that they wanted... My concern was that the teachers who might not have much direction would just go into the classroom and sit there and not really know what to look at. So this questioning has now evolved into three big questions... How is the teacher relating the lesson objective and the new learning to students with prior knowledge and prior learning? How is the teacher checking for understanding as the lesson proceeds? How is the teacher assessing whether or not the students have met their lesson objective?*

Working with the leadership team was just one step in Max's decision-making process. He was exceptionally thoughtful about how to roll out the initiative:

> *Our next step is to bring this whole thing to the faculty, which is about twenty other teachers… Some of the teachers on the leadership team have some ideas about how to get this done, about how to present this information to the faculty, but there are still some big questions that remain. These are the ones that I am most nervous about. I feel, with enough time and with enough examples, people will feel pretty good about what it means to relate information to students' prior knowledge and… some techniques that teachers have done, that teachers use to do that. What are some ways that teachers are checking for understanding?*

Notice how Max openly acknowledged his emotions and concern about the potential pitfalls. Although Max was *nervous*, he was not paralyzed by his fears. Instead, he allowed his guiding principle—his desire to establish an instructional focus at the school—to keep the initiative moving forward. Max owned the fact that he did not have all the answers and that he did not fully know a clear path to achieve his intended outcome:

> *It's really hard… to work with teachers, to bring instruction to the faculty and talk to them about having post-observation conferences between the observer and observed. And how to make that time meaningful and how to make sure that teachers are being respectful of one another, using collegial language. So that's the big thing that I'm nervous about right now. I'm not sure exactly how to go about that.*

During the questioning portion of the storytelling process, Max reflected on his past experiences at other schools, and he used these learnings to guide his decision making and action-taking processes. Notice his focus on garnering buy-in and support to ensure a successful implementation of the peer-observation protocol:

> *Again, I don't want to just throw teachers in there. That's what happened at my old school. We scheduled the observations; people went and observed. And who the hell knows what happened after that? I want to give teachers some tools. I want to give them time and respect in allowing them to look at what they want to look at, but I don't just want them to go and hang out… I'm really banking a lot on the fact that so many teachers were interested in doing pre-observations at the start of the year. The buy-in should be there already.*

It is not at all surprising that when school leaders are clear about the challenges they face, when they have a clear idea of intended outcome, and when they have a clear decision-making process that authentically engages the various stakeholder groups, tension and pain-points are far less likely. As a result, there will be less strong emotion with which school leaders must contend when taking action. The heuristic in Figure 8.2 depicts the clarity of such decision-making processes.

Figure 8.2 *Challenge Calling for Action (1)*

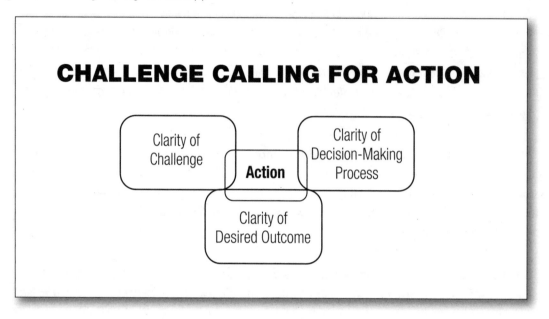

On the other hand, there are many situations in which school leaders may not be fully cognizant of the challenges they are confronting or what their intended outcome is. As previously noted, many stories told by school leaders reveal decision-making processes that are not effectively designed to address the situation at hand, or the leaders are not clear about their intended outcome. This is when a new school leader is more likely to encounter strong emotion—or to create a situation that elicits strong emotion.

Let's return to the story about Michael C. (September 2002), the high school assistant principal from Chapter 2 who confronted the student using a cell phone on campus, which almost led to a physical altercation. Initially, Michael believed that the challenge could be attributed to the student's noncompliance. When the student did not respond to his initial directive to "put [the cell phone] away," Michael's subsequent decisions and actions reflected an increasingly authoritarian, heavy-handed approach, complete with police-like language.

Eventually, with the help of the school security officer, Michael was able to get the angry student into his office. After he had a conversation with the student, Michael realized that he was initially unclear about the challenge he was confronting. The major problem was not that the young man failed to comply with his directive; the problem was that the school had given up on the student! In Michael's words:

> *[The student] had only been scheduled for four classes and informed of a proficiency test that he could take in November that would enable him to get out of high school... So it was pretty clear to me that... the school had given up on him.*

In another story that reveals how a lack of metacognitive practices can elicit intense emotion, Debbie M. (October 2003)—the elementary school assistant principal from Chapter 3—was charged with addressing the "custodial problem" at her school. Although Debbie readily communicated her desired outcome—to improve the cleanliness of the school—she failed to consider the consequences of following the district procedures exactly as they were written. She lacked a clear decision-making process, and she failed to involve the relevant stakeholders.

When one of the custodians in her school went on long-term disability, the district never provided a substitute custodian. The district had a policy whereby administrators were expected to fill out a form when rooms were not cleaned; however, these forms were not intended for use when a custodian was absent. After submitting a rash of forms, Debbie received an angry phone call from the superintendent:

> "Why are we getting all these forms? Why aren't you writing these people up?" And then I started to say something, and she stopped me and said, "You're not listening to me." And she goes right on screaming… I knew she just needed to rage.

Debbie claimed that she was merely following orders; yet, in reviewing her decision-making process, it becomes clear that she never checked—formally or informally—with any of her superiors to learn the best way to rectify the situation.

For a final example of a story that shows the importance of engaging in metacognitive processes, recall Gretchen C. (November 2002)—the high school assistant principal from Chapter 6—who had physically redirected a student. When talking with the student's mother, Gretchen remained polite and was "Ma'am-ing her to death."

> I started to say something and she said, "My name is not Ma'am. My name is blah blah blah. What's your name? Billy? Bob? Pat?" At which point I was, like, coming out of my chair… She's really angry at me. And I'm still assuming it's over this incident. And when she did the "Billy, Bob, Pat," I'm like, oh. Oh, I see where we're going on this. This is a gay thing.

Gretchen identified one of the challenges that she was facing: that of discrimination based on her sexual orientation. Gretchen was very clear that she wanted to take some kind of action. In the very beginning of her story, Gretchen told her listeners that she had filed a sexual harassment complaint. Her decision to do so was very clear. Interestingly, when the questioner asked Gretchen what she expected the district to do, Gretchen responded, very heatedly, "I don't know. I don't know. Let them figure that out!" Gretchen readily acknowledged that she was unclear about the intended outcome. As a result, she did not consider how she might find personal or professional resolution to a repugnant problem.

We now have the makings of a new graphical representation of what might happen when there is a low level of awareness regarding the challenge being faced, when there is no clarity regarding the intended outcome, or when a thoughtful decision-making process is lacking. Under such circumstances, the school leader is likely to experience, or become the target of, intense emotion (see Figure 8.3).

Figure 8.3 *Challenge Calling for Action (2; with "intense emotion")*

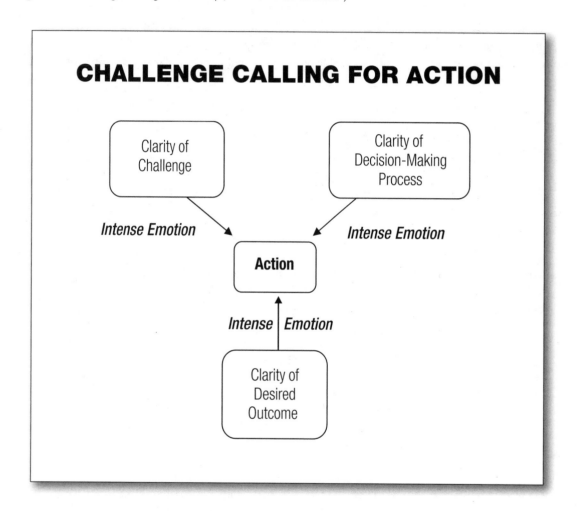

CONFLUENCE OR CONFLICT

Unfortunately, the development of metacognitive processes will not necessarily prevent a school leader from encountering intense emotion. Additional forces in the school setting that can elicit strong feelings include institutional responsibilities, stakeholder expectations, and guiding principles (these influences were detailed in Chapter 7).

As previously noted, *guiding principles* are the personal values that school leaders hold most closely to their hearts. They represent how many leaders define themselves as school leaders. A myriad of guiding principles are shared in leadership narratives, and site administrators express a profound concern for upholding these principles. The most common values expressed by new school leaders include

- good teaching and learning (16 percent)

- student centeredness (13 percent)

- equity (10 percent)

- collaboration and community (6 percent)

- safety (5 percent)

- honesty and integrity (5 percent)

- rules and compliance (4 percent)

Institutional responsibilities include the norms and expectations that come with being a site-level administrator. Some of these expectations are unwritten, whereas others are expressed in the form of an actual job description or a school or district policy. In addition, school leaders are expected to uphold the education codes and the laws of their state. In total, there are more than 20,000 education codes or laws that pertain to children and dictate the ways in which minors are treated within our educational institutions. Examples include very specific district policies for how children with special needs will be educated; codes such as Education Code (EC) 48900, which delineates detailed criteria for suspension and expulsion; and codes that are more vague and apply to the personal conduct of educators (known as "moral turpitude").

Last, but certainly not least, are the various *expectations of the stakeholders* in the school community, which include—but are not limited to—students, teachers, parents, co-administrators, site-level administrators, community members, community business leaders, and special interest groups. Although the general public agrees that students should graduate with a high school diploma, it is not unusual for conflicts to emerge among various constituencies about *what* skills and knowledge students should acquire, *how* they should be taught, and under what conditions the teaching and learning should occur.

Sometimes these three forces are in confluence; they comfortably overlap and offer a unified call for a course of action. In such situations, harmony is more likely in the school environment, and there may be little conflict for the school leader to address. Under these conditions, it is easy to make decisions or take action (see Figure 8.4).

Other times, profoundly different hopes and expectations come into play; under these circumstances, the educational leader is expected to act, intervene, and decide between passionately different courses of action. It is in this type of scenario that intense emotions are likely to emerge.

Figure 8.4 *Challenge Calling for Action (3; Venn diagram version)*

Many school leaders describe strong emotion in their narratives when a discrepancy occurs between the institutional expectations and their guiding principles. A good example of this was when Henry K., the middle school assistant principal from Chapter 3, attempted to hire a special education teacher who had been given a bad recommendation in the district. Henry was excited to have found an African American man who wanted a teaching position and had a degree in special education, one of the teaching areas with the most severe shortages. Very quickly, however, Henry learned that this particular teacher had been "released" by another principal in the district, meaning that he was ineligible for rehire. After some reflection and soul-searching, Henry decided that he was not going to passively accept the institutional expectations—in this case, the human resources policy:

> *I said, okay, I just can't let this go. I cannot let this go. So I immediately e-mailed [the principal] saying, "Look, this is our population. These kids have been denied so much in their lives. The only thing they have right now is this school. So, what can we do to turn this school around, make it so that it's the one thing they look forward to during the day?... She doesn't e-mail me back, so the next morning I call her; I say, "I have to talk to you. Drop what you're doing."*

Ultimately, the principal agrees to look into the matter, and Henry is given a shard of hope that he may have influenced a positive outcome for his students. The principal eventually gets back to Henry and says, "You can't hire him... because he's known. He's been marked. He's been blacklisted." Henry examined his guiding principles and resignedly came to the realization that there were no satisfactory options left to him. In his reflections, he shared the anguish that comes when a school leader's core values conflict with institutional policies and expectations:

> *I thought to myself… "Am I strong enough to do that right now?" I've been here four weeks—how do I push for this? How do you override not just one principal, but another very powerful principal in the district, and the district office, to get someone in who might be able to do some good at this school?… What to do now? Um, that's kind of what I'm struggling with here. You know, part of me says, well… what do I have to lose? Just put me back in the classroom.*

Finally, there are circumstances in which the institutional responsibilities bump up against the expectations of stakeholders. Recall Darlene D. (February 2003)—the middle school assistant principal from Chapter 7—who shared a story in which she faced just such incongruity:

> *[I'm dealing with] an incident in our school where a sixth-grade, emotionally disturbed student pushed a teacher. The teacher happened to be eight months pregnant… I think that, yeah, we were in the wrong for not showing that teacher how to deal with him… [We are now considering if we will expel or allow him to come] back to our school.*

Darlene was expected to navigate this horrific situation, and she allowed herself to be guided by her job responsibilities, which—plain and simple—called for an expulsion. When she considered the two primary stakeholder groups, students and teachers, the need to expel became all the more apparent. The students needed to see that one of their peers could not "get away" with such a transgression, and the teachers had to feel that their safety needs were being met. In that sense, Darlene's institutional expectations were in line with her institutional responsibilities. As she wrestled with how to resolve the situation, she reflected on yet another stakeholder—the father of the emotionally disturbed student, who argued, "What [my son] did was wrong, yes, but I don't think the school did anything to keep him from going down this route. I don't think the teacher handled the situation correctly." Adding fuel to the fire, the special education teachers argued that a student should not face consequences for a behavior that was directly connected to his disability.

Ultimately, Darlene needed to make a decision, and she found an alternative placement for the student; she fulfilled her institutional responsibilities to expel the student. Although she expressed uneasiness about giving up on a student, she rationalized this decision by explaining that the student would not have been given a fair shake by the teachers had he been allowed to return to the school. Needless to say, tremendous emotion pulsed throughout the school community as this decision was being made.

Finally, in some situations a school leader's guiding principles can conflict with stakeholder expectations. Recall Mark C. (May 2003), the high school assistant principal from Chapter 5, who made the discovery that there was a concerted effort among some of the honors teachers to arbitrarily limit access to honors classes.

> *So who gets into these honors sections is what I started to take a look at… However, the issue is in English… And what I found out is that they have a quota system. The quota system was pretty*

much based on the number of sections that this department wanted to offer. So it didn't have anything to do with a student's ability... So they were capping the total... And I uncovered this kind of acciden- tally, because all of a sudden I heard there was going to be a list that was going to be posted and only the kids on the list were going to be allowed in. In fact, the data clerk was telling me that every year she gets the list and then she pulls all of the kids out of honors classes if they're not on this magic list... and it was disjointed.

Here, Mark expressed his guiding principles through his actions. He took the necessary steps to ensure that more students would gain access to the honors courses (and the extra grade point average), thereby providing greater opportunities for college admission.

And then I looked at how many students had signed up, and over 130 students had signed up. So we were talking about bumping out close to 40 kids from this honors class. And so I said, "Wow, that's a big discrepancy here... 130 kids have signed up. How are we going to kick these kids out?" And then I started going, wait a minute, I can run a report that [shows] grade distribution by course. So I can see how many As and Bs there were in the different classes. And imagine this, in our honors section classes alone, there were 107 students who got an A or a B. So, if you just use common sense, none of these formulas and assessments and tests... if a student gets an A or a B in the freshman honors class, why shouldn't they be allowed to continue?... So where did the 90 come from?

The range of emotions expressed in the story was extraordinary. First, Mark was outraged, but after formulating a plan of action, he became elated. When he confronted the department chair, she initially expressed anger and then embarrassment:

And it was pretty sad. The reaction was... they felt like they had been exposed... And it had been going on for twenty years... She pretty much completely backpedaled once the data was put before her... I did inform her that at a minimum there's 144 students who definitely have rights, so we're not going to be placing any lists and so forth.

During this part of the storytelling process, Mark became animated when he shared his discovery and the corresponding actions he took with the superintendent. Toward the end of the process, and with prodding from his colleagues, Mark softened his stance a little bit and began to contemplate the profound responsibility he had to give feedback and facilitate change as an instructional leader. Notice, again, the tremendous swings in emotional affect:

I started to get weak. I mean, usually I'm pretty loud; sometimes I'm a little too boisterous. I actually saw myself starting to backpedal. It was uncomfortable; I'll be honest with you. And usually I'm pretty confident, and maybe can feel tough, but then when I've got this person who's been teaching for twenty-something years... I like her as a person, and as a first-year administrator I'm telling her "you may be able to get away with this"... And so I was caught where I didn't want to be so forceful because I wanted, in the moment, to tell her her business, but then I worried about the mutiny and the relationships, and really if they stop respecting your work and working with you, it can be hell. But at the same time I knew I was right. And I said that I felt that I was right. So how do you push forward without alienating and causing the staff to rebel?… I didn't want the conflict. I didn't want the confrontation. But I stuck with it. 🙶

   🙷 🙷 🙷 🙷 🙷

From listening to the stories that new leaders tell, it becomes apparent that the greater the discrepancy in guiding principles, institutional responsibilities, and stakeholder expectations, the greater the likelihood that the school leader will experience intense emotion. In addition to those situations that call for action, there are a variety of conflicts that may be of no direct concern to the school leader. For example, conflicts may exist between parents and teachers, between custodians and secretaries, and between students and teachers. When school leaders attempt to resolve one of these conflicts, they can easily become the target of the anger and frustration. Figure 8.5 depicts the emergence of intense emotions when the aforementioned forces do not converge.

Figure 8.5 *Challenge Calling for Action (4; Venn with "intense emotion")*

This heuristic is not particularly difficult to understand. However, by overlaying the two graphics that represent the triggers to intense emotion, the complexity of administrative decision making becomes much more clear. We see how easy it is to evoke intense emotion in others or to experience such emotion internally (see Figure 8.6).

Figure 8.6 *Challenge Calling for Action (5; combo of all)*

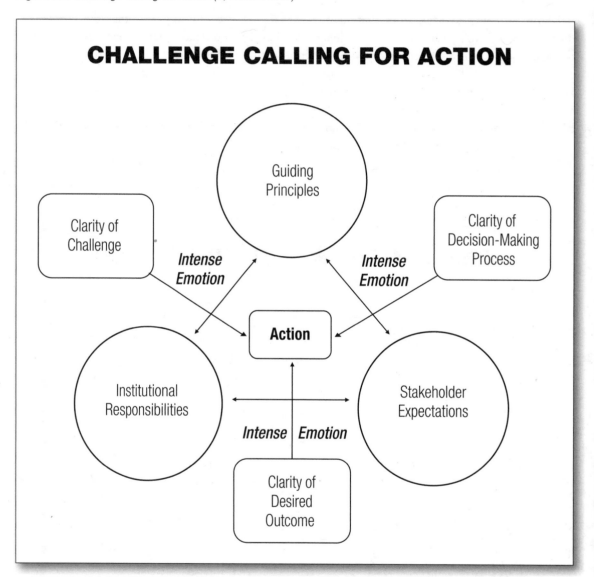

School leaders can use the reflective storytelling process and this corresponding graphic to pinpoint the intersection of causal factors that contribute to intense emotion. They can then reevaluate their decisions and courses of action and consider whether there is anything that they might do differently when managing future complex situations. This heuristic can make the challenges more understandable, transparent, and predictable. Recognizing the potential triggers will not enable school leaders to avoid tension or strong emotion altogether; rather, this tool provides an opportunity for school leaders to better anticipate reactions and plan their responses to intense emotion before it emerges. It can encourage leaders to consider different alternatives when making a decision, to think about possible areas of compromise, or to redesign their decision-making process altogether.

From reading the body of narratives shared by school leaders, one is likely to assume that the school environment is exploding with one emotionally volatile situation after another. Although an extraordinary number of challenges do exist in the school setting, not every moment is emotionally charged. Indeed, an enormous amount of paperwork, correspondence, budgetary considerations, and pleasant social interactions occur each and every day on the school campus and in the classrooms.

However, given the fact that school leadership involves a steady stream of work with frustrated, angry, marginalized students, teachers, parents, and community members, school leaders must learn to deal not only with matters of the head but with matters of the heart as well. It is interesting to note that other professionals understand the importance of providing direct training to deal with emotions.

> [Certified flight instructors] attend not only to skill but also to perception and emotion. They teach pilots what instruments and feelings to trust, and which to ignore. They help pilots learn to "fly the plane," ignoring distraction and emotion. They attend to the stress and fear that often accompany flight instruction. (Bloom et al. 2005, 6)

Why are pilots, who are learning to operate a machine, given training in how to work with their emotions, while school leaders—who are expected to work with spirited students, teachers, parents, community members, and other administrators—are given the school site plan, some theoretical instruction, an administrative credential, and a proverbial pat on the back? School leaders are expected to control and marshal their emotions amid a cacophony of conflicting expectations in order to make decisions and take actions, all while setting the tone and allocating scarce resources. Regularly, they become the focal point of anger and frustration from various stakeholders throughout the school community, and they must learn to effectively manage the tensions and navigate the intense emotions that continually come frothing to the surface of their work.

Reflective Questions for Prospective and Practicing School Leaders

❧ What do you believe are some of the root causes of the strong emotion that you have observed in your school setting?

❧ How is emotion generally expressed in your school community? Are there norms and expectations for talking about controversial issues?

❧ What typically triggers a strong emotional response in you?

❧ What have been some of your ineffective, inappropriate, or unproductive responses to these triggers?

❧ What are some of the effective strategies that you use when you are particularly angry, frustrated, or disappointed?

❧ Are there individuals or groups of individuals who need strong facilitation and close monitoring when they come together?

❧ Who are the heroes, villains, and fools in your school community?

❧ What are the most effective strategies you have used to work with angry and agitated individuals?

❧ Is there a difference in the way you interact with students, teachers, and parents who are upset?

❧ Who do you have in your professional life that provides you with structured opportunities to reflect on the challenges and emotions you encounter in the workplace?

Chapter 9

INHABITING THE ROLE OF SCHOOL LEADER:

The Principal as Superhero

It is Stories of Identity—narratives that help individuals think about and feel who they are, where they are from, and where they are headed—that constitutes the single most powerful weapon in the leader's literary arsenal.

Howard Gardner, 1995

Moving out of the classroom and into the role of site administrator is not an easy transition, but the identity of a new school leader can be informed and developed through a process of reflective storytelling within a professional learning community. The cape of leadership is what the participants wear on the school campus every day; storytelling provides an opportunity to examine who they are becoming and how comfortably the clothes of leadership are worn. Identity construction can be found at the intersection of role playing, decision making, and meaningful-making; an authentic leader must learn to integrate matters of the head, hands, and heart and to continually refine and align thoughts, words, and actions. Reflective practitioners will continually ask themselves, "Who am I as a school leader?" This is not such an easy question to answer.

Who you are as a school leader is defined by where you have been and what you have done. It is also influenced by where you are now, where you are heading, and how you are working to get there. Who you are as a school leader is expressed by what you stand for and what you will not tolerate. It is also molded by the expectations you set for yourself and others. Who you are as a school leader is defined by how you work with others and how you create the conditions so that they can learn and grow as leaders in their own right. Who you are as a school leader is shaped by how you reflect and evolve.

Although some freshly credentialed administrators are quite comfortable jumping headfirst into a principalship, others have deliberately chosen to remain far away from site administration for a period of time, seeking out more than one coaching relationship and even participating in more than one induction program before leaping into the fray. The assistant principalship and the role of dean are two of the more common entry-level positions into the world of educational administration. These positions afford the new school leader the opportunity to obtain support and guidance as the new body of skills and knowledge are being developed. Alexis (October 2002), a new assistant principal, described the "luxury" of playing a subordinate role:

> *As an assistant principal, it's easy. It's like a leader and a follower. So I still have that cushion. If all goes wrong, you can talk to… the principal. It's a luxury as an assistant principal. We lead as assistant principal, but we also follow. So it's a comforting position to be in.*

In other situations, it can be extraordinarily uncomfortable serving beneath the shadow of an ineffective or oppressive supervisor. Of the 246 narratives we collected, 17 (7 percent) described a conflict with the direct supervisor. It is not surprising that, when dealing with ineffective, absentee, or unsupportive supervisors, school leaders generally expressed low feelings of efficacy. Although good supervisors can establish positive and effective coaching relationships, the fact that a direct supervisor is charged with the responsibility of evaluating, hiring, and firing means that the supervisee may be less than open in sharing his or her more poignant difficulties and challenges. Unfortunately, few school leaders get to decide who their boss will be, especially when they are first starting out. Sandy S. (October 2003), a vice principal, explained her plight:

> *And I think, for me, right now it's hard for me to be in this role… I'm under him. And I'm really not used to that. So what I'm having to do is monitor myself, not to say too much, to take on too big of a role, to be somewhat—not subservient, but I have to realize that I do have a boss and he's not a particularly collaborative kind of person, which is making it a lot more difficult. He's very top-down directed. He tries to control everything, so trying to find a way to work with him has been a challenge. So what I find myself doing is, when I'm talking to him, trying not to make him defensive. Try to open your lines of communication, but it's a really difficult thing to do. So I think that this role of being sort of second-in-command is a really hard role for me. And I think it's a challenge that I'm starting to figure out slowly.*

Fortunately, in most situations, assistant principals are able to rely on their principal to take the heat and shield them from the political maelstrom as they develop their own identity and figure out how to play the various roles expected of them. It takes some time to fully understand what it means to be an enforcer, a system builder, an equity promoter, an instructional leader, and a person who is able to make decisions, navigate intense emotion, and get things done. When a plant is re-potted, it is not at all unusual for it to wither for a period of time before resuming its growth pattern.

When John K. (September 2004)—a new assistant principal—asked one of his more experienced colleagues (a three-year veteran) how he could possibly learn the details, legalities, and politics of his new position, the colleague suggested, "Just fake it 'til you make it!" John was neither satisfied nor amused.

SenseMaking: The Ambiguity of School Leadership

Activity and meaning are loosely coupled: events have multiple meanings because people inter-pret experience differently... People create symbols [and stories] to resolve confusion, increase predictability, provide direction, and anchor hope and faith.

—Lee Bolman and Terrence Deal, 1997

The role of school leader can be particularly amorphous, regardless of the specificity found in a job description. Most new leaders come to the role after serving as a teacher in a traditional school setting in which a bell rings every fifty minutes or so, the master schedule dictates *when* each subject will be taught, and the state standards dictate *what* will be taught. Sometimes there are even mandates about *how* things will be taught. The day in the life of the school administrator is profoundly different—there is enormous flexibility coupled with tremendous responsibility.

The common roles and activities that new leaders described were explored in chapters 2–5; however, in reviewing the 246 narratives, I identified a set of narratives that did not seem to fit into a specific category. After digging a little deeper into these stories, it became clear that there was a common focus, a common role that was indeed being played: that of sense maker. In fact, 29 of the narratives (12 percent) described new administrators struggling to understand the responsibilities and expectations associated with their new position and working to grasp what was happening in the field around them. Many new administrators were gathering information to define their role, get a read on the faculty or the community, or better comprehend the nature and nuance of a challenge that called for action. The stories yielded reflections on the motivations of key stakeholders, unwritten institutional expectations, and an internal process of values clarification.

Some novice administrators are very uncomfortable with the ambiguity of the role and take decisive action to create some coherence and clarify the execution of their professional responsibilities. Monica C. (September 2004), a middle school assistant principal, passionately described her challenge:

> " *So last Monday, I asked the assistant superintendent for my job description—I had a meet-ing with him. And he said, "I'll have it ready for you when you come in on Monday." And I was sitting there waiting and waiting. And he was like, "Well, it's lost. It's been misplaced. As soon as it turns up I'll give it to you." And I'm like, "Okay, great." [The principal asks me] "What do you think your job should be?" I said, "I have some responsibilities in the school." I'm the SST coordinator and scheduler, and I schedule all the IEP and 504 meetings, and I communicate with the parents and the teachers and everything about those meetings. I teach a pre-algebra eighth-grade class. And I co-teach a targeted*

instruction reading class... I'm really frustrated. And I'm like, "Is this what leadership is like? We just make up our own jobs. We just do what we think we should be doing." I told her, "I need the piece of paper. If you just tell me what I'm responsible for, then I could figure it out"... And then she tells me, "It's okay for a few months if you shadow me and just get the feeling for things." And I said, "I can't really do that, because people are coming to me. Parents are coming to me. Teachers are asking me questions. Students are coming to me, asking me things. And I feel I should know. And it's just really, really frustrating.

This is a rich narrative in that it accurately captures the frantic pace of administration, and it shows how challenging it can be to stop, plan, and reflect when new issues emerge and relentlessly demand the attention of the school leader. Although it may be reasonable to expect a written job description that details specific roles and responsibilities, as one new leader pointed out, "Did you ever notice that at the bottom of every job description they include the statement 'and all duties as assigned'?" Being new to the position and the school site—and being unclear of the roles, responsibilities, and expectations—can indeed be highly stress inducing. It takes time and experience to comfortably assume the identity of a school leader.

Kouzes and Posner showed how such ambiguity can impact one's physiology in their study of soldiers who were vying for positions in an elite military unit. Each of four groups was informed that it would be required to participate in a "forced march." The first team was told it would be marching twelve miles, and the soldiers were given detailed information about their progress along the way. The second group simply was told that it was doing a big march, and the soldiers received no updates along the way. The third team initially was told that it would be marching nine miles; however, with less than one mile to go, the soldiers were told they had to hike an extra four miles. The final group was told that it would be hiking eighteen miles, but at the eight-mile mark, the soldiers were informed that they had only three and a half miles to complete the march. Each of the participants was given a blood test to measure his or her stress level (the amount of cortisol and prolactin). Not surprisingly, the first group—which had the most accurate information and the most frequent updates of progress—fared the best. The team that fared the worst was the second group, which received the least amount of information about both the hike length and their progress (Kouzes and Posner 1987). One can safely assume that novice school leaders who have incomplete information about their roles, responsibilities, and corresponding progress have significant amounts of cortisol and prolactin coursing through their veins!

To better control their stress levels, some new leaders begin the process of identity formation by highlighting the job responsibilities that they don't like—those that are not in line with their personal guiding principles. Sandy S. began to craft a plan that might enable her to avoid those activities that do not fit in with her construct of the position:

One of the roles that I'm expected to play as the vice principal is the role of crime investigator. I hate this. I hate this job. All the rest of the vice principal stuff, including the discipline stuff,

I don't really mind it. But these days I'm excited when I get a straightforward referral... and I can talk to the kid and I can contact the parents and do some appropriate vaguely educationally related follow-up. Who broke into so-and-so's locker and stole the purse and then threw it in the garbage? What does this have to do with my job? Why do I care? And why should I? And why am I investigating this when there's a perfectly good police officer sitting across the hall from me who was trained in this and might possibly give a damn about the outcome of this investigation, because I don't! I don't have the skills for this. But it's much like men and laundry. I don't want skills for this; otherwise, I'll have to do it all the time.

It is unlikely that Sandy will have the luxury of avoiding the traditional job responsibilities of an assistant principal. However, this may be the beginning stages of a school leader who will prioritize and pursue those activities that she believes are most meaningful.

In the process of identity formation, many school leaders express frustration when they learn that their job responsibilities may prevent them from engaging in those activities that they deem to be most important. Administrators are no longer the direct service providers to students; they are no longer on the front lines. It is now their duty to ensure that other members of the school community are effectively serving the students. Maya T. (September 2004), an elementary school principal, described her compulsion to directly help and connect with students:

I'm running the cafeteria, 11:30–12:30, and I'm checking the students... And there are a lot of things that happen in the cafeteria... I want to connect with the children... For example, one child had to throw up. And instead of just thinking as a principal, like, "What... people [are] available here?"... I want to take [care of] the student... So for me, it's a challenge to not do that... When you are a principal, it seems like it's different.

The process of identity formation does not take place overnight. The compulsion to clean up after others, tutor children, or play a counseling role with students runs deep. One new leader talked about his challenge in conducting teacher observations, during which he fought the urge "to march to the front of the class, grab the chalk out of the teacher's hand, and teach those kids the way it's supposed to be done." Needless to say, this probably would not have been well received by the teacher being observed.

Just figuring out the responsibilities and expectations of the new position—just getting to know the individuals in the school community who can help and those who can hurt—can take the better part of a year. The learning curve is incredibly steep. The melding of institutional expectations and personal values can make the walk and talk of the novice school leader present as stilted, unnatural, and uncomfortable. But, over time, many novice school leaders do find ways to construct an authentic identity and walk comfortably and effectively throughout all corners of the school community.

MEANINGFUL-MAKING

I'm standing on the edge of some crazy cliff. What I have to do, I have to catch everybody if they start to go over the cliff—I mean if they're running and they don't look where they're going I have to come out from somewhere and catch them. That's all I'd do all day. I'd just be the catcher in the rye and all.

—*Holden Caulfield,* Catcher in the Rye *(J. D. Salinger, 1951)*

Engaging in a process of reflective storytelling is not just about meaning-making; it is also about "meaningful-making." I coined this phrase as a means of encouraging new leaders to ask themselves continually, "How do I find meaning in the work I am expected to do?" All school leaders need opportunities to reflect on the meaningfulness of their work and to reframe the challenges and their corresponding actions so that the work can present as an expression of personal values. The decisions that school leaders make and the actions they take—the culmination of words, expressions, and actions—combine to form an image, a symbol that members of a school community readily hold on to.

The actions and symbols of leadership frame and mobilize meaning. Leaders articulate and define what has previously remained implicit or unsaid; then they invent images, metaphors, and models that provide a focus for new attention. By so doing, they consolidate or challenge prevailing wisdom. In short, an essential factor *in leadership is the ability to influence and* organize meaning *for the members of the organization. (Bennis and Goldsmith 1997, 104)*

It is not unusual for students and teachers to report principal "visitations" in their dreams. Reflective school leaders regularly ask themselves, "What do I represent to those with whom I work? What kind of image am I cultivating? What values am I expressing?"

Initially, the desire to find meaning in the work can be overshadowed by the desire to look good or, at the very least, to avoid looking foolish. Jenny M. (September 2004), a first-year elementary school principal, described her first steps walking in leadership shoes. This narrative was shared in September, at which point Jenny had been on the job for less than one month:

> *And I thought, "Oh." I just didn't want to have to seem like I was following somebody else. I didn't want to fill anyone's shoes. I have my own shoes. I thought, "How am I going to present myself in a way that I call respect?" or demand respect or whatever word you want to say, but not be rude about it and not step on anyone's toes and just come in gracefully if I could, because I have a tendency to stumble in on things.*

There is a profound need to find meaning in the work that we do. Some school leaders describe their work as being mission driven, whereas others assert that education is a social responsibility. Still others talk about their work as having a spiritual component:

> *The biggest challenge for me at the beginning of the year was, and continues to be, figuring out the universe's plan for me and why I ended up where I am. Because, on a spiritual level, I can talk about that. I am the assistant principal of curriculum at one of the largest high schools in the district, which means basically I sit in an office and I have very little contact with kids—minimal. And sometimes not at all… except to tell a kid to take his hat off in the hallway when I'm doing hall supervision. This is not why I went into education. This is not feeding my soul, and I knew that when I was given the position… There's a lesson for me to learn here. (Anne T., September 2004)*

This is what reflective practitioners do: they question, they reflect, they struggle, and they search for meaning over and over again. The process of taking ownership of identity in a new role—the process of becoming effective as a school leader—is just that: a continual process of *becoming*.

THE TENSIONS IN SCHOOL LEADERSHIP

Yield and overcome;

Bend and be straight;

Empty and be full;

Wear out and be new;

Have little and gain;

Have much and be confused…

Be really whole,

And all things will come to you.

—*Lao Tsu,* Tao Te Ching

Making decisions and taking action require a deep understanding of the needs and desires of the competing stakeholders, the various influences, and the core values that permeate the field. At each turn, the school leader is expected to make explicit where he or she resides along the various continuua related to school leadership. No wonder the process of identity construction is such a difficult process: walking the tightrope of school leadership requires incredible dexterity, courage, and commitment. Demonstrating poise and balance under the big top is part of the artistry of serving as a school leader.

Many tensions exist in the world of educational leadership. Just as there is discord between theory and practice in the larger field of education, there is also tension regarding the need to apply the appropriate balance of pressure and support. Researched-based, "scientific" strategies guide effective decision making and leadership, but there is also an artistry that requires graceful social interactions, feedback, and facilitation. A school leader must balance inquiry with advocacy. Leaders whose advocacy is too strong or passionate may be seen as bulls in a china shop; however, if an inquiry stance is used too frequently, the leader will be seen as weak and indecisive.

An effective leader also must maintain an appropriate balance between listening and communicating, reflection and action. School leaders must work as actors in the unfolding drama of school leadership, readily jumping into the role of critic, confronting the disheartening data, and having hard conversations in which they must trust their judgment and speak their truth. At times, they will be expected to do the grunt work of a mild-mannered reporter, whereas at other times, they will be called on to play the role of superhero. Figure 9.1 is a list of tensions found in the literature, uncovered in the stories, and observed in the field of the school leader.

Figure 9.1 *Tensions in School Leadership*

Remain mindful of educational and learning theory.	Focus on practice and that which works in the field.
Build intimacy and cultivate a caring and nurturing school community (offer support).	Push, challenge, question, and confront (apply pressure).
Create informal, open, flexible, participant-driven learning communities (Little 2002; Lave and Wenger 1991).	Create institutionalized structures, protocols, and processes within a professional learning community (Palinscar and Brown 1984).
Focus on the art of teaching, learning, and leading.	Focus on the science of teaching, learning, and leading.
Promote collaborative inquiry (Senge 1990).	Engage in passionate advocacy (Senge 1990).
Focus on process.	Focus on outcomes.
Listen.	Communicate.
Engage in theory acquisition.	Engage in theory development.
Focus on theory and reflection.	Focus on practice and action.
Work as an actor in the unfolding drama.	Serve as the critic.
Work as Clark Kent.	Fight like Superman!

Just as providing a heuristic that represents the triggers to intense emotion can provide new leaders with a tool to predict and plan for situations that are likely to provoke strong emotion, so too can a matrix of leadership tensions serve as a device to press school leaders to reflect on their practice and consciously situate themselves along the various continuua. Providing such a matrix does not make school leadership any easier; however, becoming more mindful of the tensions in the field can help leaders become more thoughtful, deliberate, and metacognitive in their practice.

DEFINING SUCCESS IN LEADERSHIP GROWTH: A BUMPY ROAD FROM NOVICE TO EXPERT

Prompting school leaders to look inside the mirror rather than out the window is more organic and strengthens the capacity for self-actualization. A well-facilitated process leads people beyond the war stories until they ultimately realize that their own handling of situations is actually perpetuating some of the overload.

—Suzette Lovely, 2006

The stories shared by new school leaders effectively capture the way they reflect on their work, learn, make meaning, and conceptualize their practice. When school leaders engage in a process of analyzing their own narratives, they increase their understanding of the challenges they face, the stakeholders they impact with their decisions, the principles they uphold, and the outcomes they strive to achieve. There are strong indications that participating in reflective storytelling and narrative analysis can influence the way in which new leaders think, speak, and act in the field.

In looking at the leadership narratives, some of the metacognitive terms, words, and phrases—such as *reflect, consider, analyze, review*, and *if I had to do it all over again*—appeared with great regularity. Additionally, several stories highlighted the changes that school leaders observed in their own practice, in their way of doing business, and in the way they felt about their work.

Taking the time to reflect is not easy. Rarely is there time in the course of a school day to deeply consider the nuances of a situation being handled. But the payoff can be immense. Mary J. (November 2003)—a second-year assistant principal—considered her challenges and learnings as she recalled her experience of participating in the reflective storytelling process:

> *I find it really useful. It forces me to kind of like—when you put the tape recorder on and everything—step out of the hole and kind of look down and see how to get out of it, and it pushes me to really reflect and solve my own problems. It also validates the exhaustion and fear and array of emotions that I go through, because I know that my colleagues are also experiencing stuff like that... It's pretty tough to do... but I definitely see a very good purpose in taking time to reflect... I think it's very valuable to know that I am going to be getting back to the things I reflected on. It's kind of like I want to set myself up for*

some sort of acknowledgment… on my growth at the end of the year, so I feel like I need to take the time to do that so I can visualize myself hopefully at the end of the year reading over all of my stories and going, "Yeah, we would never handle it that way again. I learned something" [laughs]. ""

In another example, Karen M. (November 2004)—a second-year assistant principal—was questioned about how she responded differently in her first year as an administrator:

"" *I would be second-guessing myself at times even though my intuition is clear… When I first started, I just had that inner wrestling with myself—am I paying attention to everything that I need to pay attention to? And that's what's depleting… [and now] I just feel much more confident because I have more things to draw upon in the toolbox.* ""

Notice the big-picture thinking and feelings of efficacy that Karen described in her reflections. Karen was proud of the greater repertoire of tools at her disposal; she was clearer about what her choices and actions might be when challenging situations present themselves.

Likewise, Gretchen C. (September 2002) engaged in a similar process of self-reflection. Initially, she described leadership as "dancing backward in high heels," but she reflected on how she has changed after serving as an assistant principal for two years:

"" *I think I know my dance partners a lot more now, and I get to dance with a lot more people… I know the stage, I know the scenery. I know what's going on better. I'm feeling more connected and in control in the second year.* ""

The metaphorical thinking that is used by these administrators is an active form of framing, conceptualizing, and integrating the work of school leadership. It is clear that creating a space for reflection—providing an opportunity to step out of prescribed roles and consider the trajectory of learning—can be of high value for school leaders. The work of administration is taxing, and it makes it somehow more manageable for new leaders when they see that they are becoming more thoughtful, confident, and effective in their practice.

The narratives shared by new school leaders offer riveting story lines, beautiful foreshadowing, and a few nail-biting climaxes. What was most surprising was that 186 of the stories (77 percent) did not have resolution! The frequency of such incomplete stories does not at all paint a picture of incompetent school leaders. Rather, such unfinished stories indicate a willingness of new administrators to use the reflective storytelling process to explore troubling situations, and to consider how they might resolve a particular quandary and authentically embody the role of school leader. Within a professional learning community, participants do not feel the need to portray themselves as superheroes who are able to effectively solve every problem that materializes in their schools.

Of course, another factor that may contribute to the number of open-ended stories is the fact that resolution often comes very slowly in the school setting. This, then, may be an important lesson for new school leaders: patience is of paramount importance for practitioners.

LESSONS FOR NEW LEADERS

There is frequently a chasm between what we know to be the best action and what we do. The connection tissue is often the courage to act.

—*Alan Blankenstein, 2004*

Many patterns emerge in the stories that new leaders tell, and many common pitfalls are shared that beg to be documented and exploited by the practitioner who has the desire to learn from others' missteps. New leaders often are eager to share their personal insights and findings in the stories they tell:

> As a vice principal, you really get callous and develop a shell, or you quit or you wish you'd get fired… I don't want to sound so bleak to anybody who may be listening to me. But there are ways to create a balance, and there are so many things that have surprised me and scared me… I'm going to continue to do what I feel is right, what I feel is the right thing to do… Anybody in this place can do whatever they want to me as long as I keep doing the right thing… what were the two promises I made? I can't indulge myself with the money issue, so I won't have to worry about getting fired. And I can't indulge the pride issue. (Steven G., May 2004)

This passage could easily be included as an example of meaningful-making or identity formation. And yet, the message that Steven wants other new leaders to get is the importance of "doing the right thing." Steven shares the empty motivators for him, which include money and status. But he reminds both himself and his colleagues that the higher calling of being principle driven can be helpful in guiding new school leaders.

Development of reflective practices is integral to moving along the continuum from novice to expert. After making a few mistakes and neglecting a few stakeholders, new leaders can and do become more strategic in gathering relevant information and making sense of their environment:

> For me, this year has been more… I come real stealthy. I just observe, collect my data. I don't say anything. I don't form any opinions… This is how I am as a person; once what I see becomes a pattern, that's when I speak on it. Some things have become patterns already. (Allison S., September 2004)

There is significant overlap in understanding the complex process of decision making, navigating intense emotion, and forming an identity. Through storytelling and narrative analysis, new leaders are able to reflect on past experiences and bring lessons learned into play as they address new and similar challenges that emerge in the field. For the new school leader, a torrent of opportunities exists for growth and development.

Sara P. (September 2004) was settling into her first year in administration, serving as the dean of students in a high school. She began her story with a brief summary of her job responsibilities, and, soon thereafter, she identified areas of discomfort in wearing the cape of the school leader:

> *My goal for this year… is to be more comfortable with difficult conversations with my colleagues—not necessarily the students in discipline. I feel pretty comfortable with discipline. But having those hard conversations… when I'm asking a teacher to change his or her [teaching] or to critique them. That is really, really difficult for me… It's difficult because I want to be liked. I don't want to be the heavy. You can't help but be the heavy in a position that we have as school leaders. I want to be the kind of sage-like leader where I ask all the right questions and help the person I'm talking to come to the right conclusion, take the right action, by being a good questioner. And I'm not, or I don't perceive myself as being that way… you shouldn't really care necessarily what people think about you. As long as you can sleep at the end of the day. [As long as] you've been fair and consistent. I don't know… that's where I'm at.*

Sara does a wonderful job defining her areas of discomfort and challenge. She explains how tricky it is to give others professional feedback when she has an overarching concern about being liked. The art of having a hard conversation is a skill that is role played in many administrative preparation programs; nonetheless, it is a challenge that leaders talk about again and again in their narratives. Sara also identified yet another tension found in school leadership: the line between personal and professional boundaries and expectations. Following a series of questions and reflections, Sara validated her own feelings:

> *You're right. I'm not being unreasonable in my expectations. I'm asking them to be professional and I'm holding them accountable. My concern is that perhaps I'm not firm enough. I am very gentle. I'm tiptoeing. I need to be maybe clearer—I don't know… We do that as newbies. We personalize it.*

The fact that Sara is deeply reflecting on her leadership practice and readily identifying her growth areas shows how a novice administrator learns to assume the identity of school leader and move along the continuum from novice to expert. Sara not only has identified *what* she needs to do as a school leader, she also is clarifying *how* she needs to do it.

Magical Objects

Sometimes, uncovering the hidden themes and patterns in administrative narratives takes a very circuitous route. In my initial review of the literature on narrative analysis, I happened upon the work of Vladimir Propp (1958), who defined the common characters and themes found in Russian fairy tales. He identified thirty-one formal and fundamental elements of a tale that appear in roughly the same sequence: a major challenge or villain emerges, the hero begins his quest, a struggle ensues, a magical object appears, the villain is defeated, and the hero is transformed. As is true in most story forms, the structure provides a frame that listeners expect—a common agreement about what makes a story exciting or complete.

I began to explore how such an analytical frame might highlight institutional norms and cultural expectations. As far as the magical object was concerned, I initially was quite skeptical: I had never heard a leadership narrative in which a magical object appeared. But when I expanded my definition of *magical* to include the notion of an object having "power," I was quite surprised at what I found. One of the primary catalysts for anger and frustration, the object that became the tipping point of intense emotion, often came in the form of a letter, a note, or some kind of written document. In fact, 55 of the 246 narratives (22 percent) described a situation in which a written document became the trigger of strong emotion. Occasionally, new administrators understood that presenting a written document, such as a negative evaluation, would likely evoke some kind of intense reaction.

In numerous stories, the written document and the subsequent tempest of emotion caught the novice leader totally off guard. Leaders do not always consider that intentions can be misinterpreted easily when communicated through e-mails, written notes, or even formal letters. Laurie A. (September 2003), a new high school assistant principal, captured how a situation involving the power of a written document played itself out in her school as she assisted a colleague in work with families of truant students:

> We have [an intern] working on attendance. She put together this list of the 30 most frequently truant kids... She brought in a letter and said... we need to send this letter to notify our parents. I looked at it and I just couldn't send it. It was so badly written in addition to being unhelpful and threatening, etc.... I felt like I had to send it more or less that way, but I tweaked it... I sent it under my name, and that was a big mistake. Unsurprisingly, there were a few hysterical parents on the phone talking about how it was threatening, and how it was trying to get them in trouble for problems that their kids were having... kids with attendance problems often have really complicated things going on in their lives. But for some reason, when this letter was put in front of me, I thought, oh yeah, "bad kids." Read this; do this. And I'm just really frustrated that I couldn't connect those two pieces of knowledge in any useful way without having to make this really stupid mistake.

Once a written document is out there in the field, it can rarely be retracted. The artifact can become an enduring symbol of thoughtlessness or bad decision making. The lesson for new leaders is: be very careful what you put in writing. The power is tremendous, the potential reaction severe.

New leaders need not only informal learning opportunities with like-minded colleagues, but also structures, protocols, and processes that will afford them the opportunity to talk about that which is most challenging and meaningful to them. One of the first trials that new leaders face is an internal process of identity construction. Novice school leaders quickly learn that many components of their work may be in direct conflict with their guiding principles, especially in the areas of discipline and confronting ineffective or inappropriate educators in the field. New leaders must find their way through this foreign territory and negotiate tense situations with their own personal style, in a way that feels authentic.

Learning must begin with experience; participating in reflective storytelling and narrative analysis provides an opportunity to develop metacognitive skills and emotional intelligence, as well as the space new leaders need to make meaning out of difficult experiences. From these reflections, new leaders can develop and refine existing theories, archetypes, and heuristics, which in turn can result in changes in practice when leaders return to the field. The graphical representation in Figure 9.2 depicts this theory of professional growth and development. It begins with stories based on personal experience and results in changes in thought, word, and deed.

Figure 9.2 *Changes in Practice*

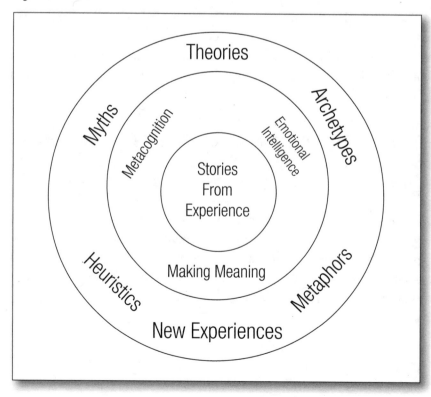

Although new leaders do not always have the latitude to choose which situations will cross their desk, they do get to choose what they say, what they do, and how they respond. They regularly choose which role they will inhabit, and how they will behave when playing a given role. The act of choosing which role to play is much more than mere nuance in school leadership. The roles we play define who we are as educational leaders, and the way we play these roles ultimately will determine our effectiveness in achieving our desired outcomes.

Success as a school leader is profoundly dependent on the ability to learn and grow. As Bennis and Goldsmith argue:

Remaining open to new learning means being truthful with ourselves and others, being willing to re-evaluate our prior beliefs in the face of new information that contradicts what we know to be true, and finally continuing to remember what is important—being clear about our priorities and our goals. (1997, 70, 104)

The expectations heaped upon the shoulders of school leaders are vast and profound. Think about Clark Kent frantically changing into the costume of Superman inside a suffocating phone booth while crises, moral dilemmas, and dangerous situations proliferate at every turn. To summarize, wearing the costume of school leader involves:

- holding students, teachers, parents, and support staff accountable for adhering to the rules, norms, and expectations of the school community (enforcer);

- addressing all of the operational needs of the school while challenging and building systems to improve efficiency and coherence (system builder);

- fulfilling one's moral imperative by promoting equity (addressing issues of racism, sexism, homophobia, etc.) and advocating for the children in the school community (equity promoter);

- driving student achievement through the improvement of teaching and learning (instructional leader);

- remaining mindful of one's personal values, stakeholder needs and expectations, and the various institutional influences and expectations;

- making good decisions and taking bold actions with thoughtful stakeholder engagement and clear decision-making processes; and

- navigating intense emotion; anticipating and responding to the emotional responses that accompany school leadership.

Reflective Questions for Prospective and Practicing School Leaders

- How do the myths of the school leader influence your ideas about how you should inhabit the role of school leader?

- What image do you represent to those in your school community?

- What skills or assets do you bring to the table as a school leader?

- What are the defining moments in your life that have influenced your ability to inhabit the role of school leader comfortably and effectively?

- What are your greatest challenges or common pitfalls that you regularly step into as a school leader? Why does this happen?

- In what ways do you solicit support for your development as a school leader?

- Who are your mentors (other superheroes) with whom you regularly interact? What have you learned from speaking with them? What have you learned from observing their behaviors?

- What messages (verbal or nonverbal) do you receive in your school community that encourage or discourage your practice as a school leader?

- What do you really want to accomplish as a school leader that would align your core values and commitment, and make you proud of your corresponding words and actions?

- What drives you as a school leader?

- What gives you the greatest satisfaction as a school leader?

- What are the areas in which you most want to evolve as a school leader during the next year? The next five years?

AFTERWORD

As I listen to these extraordinary women and men tell their life stories, I play many roles. I am a mirror that reflects back their pain, their fears, and their victories. I am also the inquirer who asks the sometimes difficult questions, who searches for evidence and patterns. I am the companion on the journey, bringing my own story to the encounter, making possible an interpretive collaboration. I am the audience who listens, laughs, weeps, and applauds. I am the spider woman spinning their tales. Occasionally, I am a therapist who offers catharsis, support, and challenge, and who keeps track of emotional mine fields [or who unwittingly steps into them]. Most absorbing to me is the role of human archeologist who uncovers the layers of mask and inhibition in search of a more authentic representation of life experience. Throughout, I must also play stage manager, coordinating the intersection of three plays—the storyteller's, the narrator's, and the reader's—inviting you to add your voice to the drama.

 Sara Lawrence-Lightfoot and Jessica Hoffman Davis, 1997

Children—even infants—love hearing stories. Their passion for story often presents as a primordial need that materializes in the form of habits, rituals, and routines. People tell stories in all cultures and all settings: at bedtime, dinnertime, social time, courting time, after unusual or threatening experiences, and—as we get older (if we are lucky)—during professional development time at work. Our need for story does not disappear when we slip into the costume of the professional. Human beings have an innate desire to learn with and from others, to be inspired, to share. This is simply what we do. It is tragic that storytelling has often been seen as a frivolous, unproductive activity; the act of sharing not only facilitates connection and caring among colleagues, it also promotes reflection and reconceptualization of past experiences, which are essential practices to continual growth and improvement.

I began this research with the premise that storytelling is a natural and comfortable activity, especially when stories are shared with like-minded colleagues who understand the trials and tribulations of being a novice school leader. Although the prompts were intended to evoke stories that describe challenging situations, they were not topically prescriptive; participants were always given the opportunity to speak on any subject that they felt was important. As such, it is my assertion that the transcribed narratives effectively capture the issues that new leaders are thinking about and wrestling with—those that keep them up at night.

The prime lesson from this research effort, then, is that storytelling is crucial to learning, growth, and the integration of new experiences. Storytelling is a process that helps new leaders make sense of their worlds. Storytelling can enable novice leaders to formulate new conceptions of how things are and how things work. Storytelling without reflection is mere entertainment; however, storytelling can serve as a springboard for professional growth and development. Reflective storytelling is all about cultivating deliberate, thoughtful, principle-driven leadership. Reflective practitioners may not always get it right, but their actions and decisions are less likely to be done thoughtlessly or impulsively.

It is evident from looking at the narratives that participating in a professional learning community can create the conditions in which nontraditional, unexpected stories can be told. In such a supportive milieu, school leaders are willing to tell the nonhero stories and even present themselves as quixotic characters lancing at windmills. The art of storytelling is of paramount importance in the day-to-day work of the school leader: "Leaders hold a sacred trust from their organization and its staff. Followers, who are often partners in an endeavor, look to leaders to interpret reality, explain the present, and paint a picture of the future" (Bennis and Goldsmith 1997, 3). Reading the administrative narratives makes it clear that most school leaders are mission driven and do have superhero-like qualities.

It is a worthy exercise to explore Superman as an extended metaphor representing the school leader. First of all, Superman was born with extraordinary abilities, but he has to make a choice—each and every day—about how he will use his special skills. As is true for all superheroes, he has an alter ego. Superman does not spend all his time flying from one crisis to another, rescuing one poor, hapless soul here and crushing another bad guy there. Even Superman needs downtime. Clark Kent—a gentle, unimposing figure—returns to his office job day after day, which allows Superman to regroup and collect himself. Kent, in the act of writing a gritty article, is able to reflect on the actions of the Caped Crusader. As an investigative reporter, Clark Kent must gather relevant information and put it on paper in a form that the public will both understand and appreciate. And, just like a school leader, Superman has tremendous difficulty maintaining balance in his life. Personal relationships are strained, and the tension of being drawn toward a higher calling is a part of his everyday existence.

Of course, school leaders are not really superheroes. They are merely passionate professionals who wear the costume of the professional and strive each day to make sure that all of the students under their watch are learning and thriving. In their own unique way, they struggle to make things a little better for students (and their families), teachers, and school communities. Their stories are important and need to be told; in fact, much can be learned from the telling of a good story.

OUTTAKES: LESSONS AND LEARNINGS FROM NEW SCHOOL LEADERS

We need leaders—neither saints nor sparkling television personalities—who can situate themselves within a larger historical narrative of this country and our world, who can grasp the complex dynamics of our peoplehood and imagine a future grounded in the best of our past, yet who are attuned to the frightening obstacles that now perplex us. Our ideals of freedom, democracy, and equality must be invoked to invigorate all of us . . . Only a visionary leadership that can motivate "the better angels of our nature," as Lincoln said, and activate possibilities for a freer, more efficient, and stable America—only that leadership deserves cultivation and support.

—West, 2001

- I've noticed that when people are screaming at you, then you tend to sit up and take notice (Debbie M., December 2003).

- Parents are still another issue. If I had 800 orphans, I'd be happy. I'd be ecstatic with 800 orphans (Ned M., September 2004).

- I don't think the district's ever had any real reward system. The only reward you get is not to get sanctioned. If you're not getting sanctioned . . . then it's all good, whatever you're doing (Henry P., September 2004).

- So I said to myself, "Okay, this is the last day of school and this is as good a day as any day to fire 11 people" (Mark K., September 2004).

- And the big lever I have for doing that is that this year I will write the master schedule. Basically I get to do whatever the hell I want, because in March anything is possible (Larry A., December 2003).

- It's not like they're going to fire me; they just hired me and I've not killed anybody yet (Peter R., December 2003).

- "I don't trust democracy" . . . I was really resistant and [the principal] said, "You have to try it even if they screw it up" (Gretchen C., December 2003).

- I was really enjoying just writing the site plan much more than I was living the day-to-day life of administering the school (Gretchen C., May 2003).

- They knew the whole time that they were going to go away and do what they wanted to do. That's the joy of administration (Alan M., May 2003).

- It's like you have to sell a really unattractive bag of nails! There's not too much rust on them, you won't get tetanus! (Sarah C., May 2003).

- I'm trying to push myself to keep finding the edge, but without becoming the queen bitch (Carrie A., September 2004).

- I don't care what your style is. If you like plaid ties, wear plaid ties. It's not a style; it is a requirement that you maintain a classroom as a professional (Steven G., April 2004).

- So I made a little ballot for modified Wednesdays that said, "Yes, I'd like to grow this year through professional development." And I made it very weighted, and the other one was, "No, I don't want to grow." We voted, and it was 10 to 4 in favor of modified Wednesdays. And I had to check handwriting and pen colors to see who voted. The lady who said to me, "And better men than you have tried" voted yes! (Peter R., September 2003).

Unless you are the lead dog, the scenery never changes.

—Anonymous

REFERENCES

Abadi, M. 2003. "'Everybody's Socializing': Narrative Structures in Stories of School Trouble." Dissertation, University of California, Berkeley.

Argyris, C. 1982. *Reasoning, Learning and Action: Individual and Organizational.* San Francisco: Jossey-Bass.

Arum, R. 2003. *Judging School Discipline: The Crisis of Moral Authority.* Cambridge, MA: Harvard University Press.

Badaracco, J., Jr. 1998. "The Discipline of Building Character." In *Harvard Business Review on Leadership.* Boston: Harvard Business School Press.

Ball, A. 1987. *The Micro-Politics of the School: Toward a Theory of School Organization.* London: Methuen.

Baquedano-Lopez, P. 1998. "Language Socialization of Mexican Children in a Los Angeles Parish." Dissertation, University of California, Los Angeles.

Barnard, C. 1938. *Functions of the Executive.* Cambridge, MA: Harvard University Press.

Barth, R. 1990. *Improving Schools from Within.* San Francisco: Jossey-Bass.

Begley, P. T. 1999. *Values and Educational Leadership.* Albany: State University of New York Press.

Bennis, W., and J. Goldsmith. 1997. *Learning to Lead: A Workbook on Becoming a Leader.* Reading, MA: Perseus Books.

Blankenstein, A. 2004. *Failure Is Not an Option.* Thousand Oaks, CA: Corwin.

Blasé, J. 1991. *The Politics of Life in Schools: Power, Conflict, and Cooperation.* Thousand Oaks, CA: Corwin.

Bloom, G., C. Castagna, E. Moir, and B. Warren. 2005. *Blended Coaching: Skills and Strategies to Support Principal Development.* Thousand Oaks, CA: Corwin.

Bolman, L. G., and T. E. Deal. 1997. *Reframing Organizations: Artistry, Choice, and Leadership.* San Francisco: Jossey-Bass.

Bransford, J. D., A. L. Brown, and R. R. Cocking. 2000. *How People Learn: Brain Mind Experience and School.* Report of the National Research Council, National Academy Press.

Bridges, E. 1992. *Problem-Based Learning for Administrators.* Eugene, OR: ERIC Clearinghouse on Educational Management.

Brown, A. 1982. "Interpersonal Administration: Overcoming the Pygmalion Effect." *Interchange* 13 (4): 15–26.

Brown, A. L., and J. C. Campione. 1996. "Psychological Theory and the Design of Innovative Learning Environments on Procedures, Principles, and Systems." In *Innovations in Learning: New Environments for Education,* ed. L. Schauble and R. Glaser. Mahwah, NJ: Lawrence Erlbaum.

Bruner, J. 1990. *Acts of Meaning.* Cambridge, MA: Harvard University Press.

———. 2002. *Making Stories: Law, Literature, Life.* Cambridge, MA: Harvard University Press.

Bryk, A., et al. 1999. *Charting Chicago School Reform: Democratic Localism as a Lever for Change.* Boulder, CO: Westview.

Champy, J. 1995. *Reengineering Management.* New York: HarperCollins.

Clandinin, D. J., and F. M. Connelly. 1991. "Narrative and Story in Practice and Research." In *Case Studies in and on Educational Practice*, ed. D. Schon. New York: Teachers College.

Clement, S. 1969. "Mr. Principal, Do You Have the Time?" *Education* 89 (2): 225–227, 69 Feb.–Mar. (ERIC No. EJ000051).

Cohen, M. D., J. D. March, and J. Olsen. 1972. "A Garbage Can Model of Organizational Choice." *Administrative Science Quarterly* 17 (1): 1–25.

Coles, R. 1989. *The Call of Stories*. Boston: Houghton Mifflin.

Collins, A., J. S. Brown, and S. E. Newman. 1989. "Cognitive Apprenticeship: Teaching the Crafts of Reading, Writing, and Mathematics." In *Knowing, Learning and Instruction: Essays in Honor of Robert Glaser*, ed. L. B. Resnick. Hillsdale, NJ: Erlbaum.

Cuban, L. 1990. "Reforming Again and Again and Again." *Educational Researcher* 19(1): 3–13.

———. 2001. *How Can I Fix It? Finding Solutions and Managing Dilemmas*. New York: Teacher's College Press.

Daley, B. J. 1999. "Novice to Expert: An Exploration of How Professionals Learn." *Adult Education Quarterly* 49 (4): 133–147.

Danzig, A. 1997. "Leadership Stories: What Novices Learn by Crafting the Stories of Experienced School Administrators. *Journal of Educational Administration* 35 (2): 122–137.

———. 1999. "How Might Leadership Be Taught? The Use of Story and Narrative to Teach Leadership." *International Journal in Education* 2 (2): 117–131.

Davis, K. 1949. *Human Society*. New York: Macmillan.

Davis, S., L. Darling-Hammond, M. LaPointe, and D. Meyerson. 2005. *School Leadership Study: Developing Successful Principals*. Palo Alto, CA: Stanford Educational Leadership Institute.

DeCuir, J. T., and Dixson, A. D. 2004. "'So When It Comes Out, They Aren't That Surprised That It Is There': Using Critical Race Theory as a Tool of Analysis of Race and Racism in Education." *Educational Researcher* (June/July): 29.

Delpit, L. 1995. *Other People's Children: Culture Conflict in the Classroom.* New York: The New Press.

DeMello, A. 1985. *One-Minute Wisdom.* Garden City, NY: Doubleday.

The Department of Education. 2001. "The Individuals with Disabilities Act Amendments of 1997." The Department of Education. http://www.ed.gov/offices/OSERS/Policy/IDEA/index.html.

Deutschman, A. 2005. *Change or Die: The Three Keys to Change at Work and in Life.* New York: HarperCollins.

Deveare Smith, A. 2000. *Talk to Me: Listening Between the Lines.* New York: Random House.

Dewey, J. 1938. *Experience and Education.* New York: Simon and Schuster.

Drucker, P. 2001. "The Effective Decision." In *Harvard Business Review on Decision Making.* Boston: Harvard Business School Press. (Orig. pub. 1967.)

DuFour, R., and R. Eaker. 1998. *Professional Learning Communities at Work.* Bloomington, IN: National Educational Service.

DuFour, R., R. Eaker, and R. DuFour. 2005. *On Common Ground.* Bloomington, IN: Solution Tree.

Dundes, A. 1965. *The Study of Folklore.* Englewood Cliffs, NJ: Prentice Hall.

Eckhartsberg, R. V. 1981. "Maps of the Mind." In *The Metaphors of Consciousness,* ed. R. S. Valle and R. V. von Eckhartsberg. New York: Plenum.

Ellinor, L., and G. Gerard. 1998. *Dialogue: Rediscover the Transforming Power of Conversation.* New York: John Wiley and Sons.

Elmore, R. F. 2000. "Building a New Structure for School Leadership." *American Educator* 23 (4): 6–13.

Epstein, J. 2001. *School, Family, and Community Partnerships.* Boulder, CO: Westview.

Etzioni, A. 2001. "Humble Decision Making." In *Harvard Business Review on Decision Making.* Boston: Harvard Business School Press. (Orig. pub. 1967.)

Feng, G., and J. English, trans. 1972. *Tao Te Ching.* New York: Vintage Books.

Ferguson, A. 2000. *Bad Boys: Public Schools in the Making of Black Masculinity.* New York: Lexington Books.

Flessa, J. 2003. "What's Urban in the Urban School Principalship: Case Studies of Four Middle School Principals in One City School District." Dissertation, University of California, Berkeley.

Foucault, M. 1977. *Discipline and Punish: The Birth of the Prison.* New York: Random House.

Fullan, M. 1993. *Change Forces: Probing the Depths of Educational Reform.* Bristol, PA: The Falmer Press.

Gardner, H. 1995. *Leading Minds: An Anatomy of Leadership.* New York: Basic Books.

Gee, J. 1999. *Discourse Analysis: Theory and Method.* London: Routledge.

Gilley, G. 1995. *Stop Managing, Start Coaching! How Performance Coaching Can Enhance Commitment and Improve Productivity.* New York: McGraw-Hill.

Goldsborough, H., et al. 1971. *The Man in the Middle: How the Urban Secondary School Principal Sees His Role and Responsibilities.* Toronto: Canadian Education Association.

Goleman, D. 1995. *Emotional Intelligence.* New York: Bantam Books.

Gonzalez, D. 1997. "Problems Faced by Beginning Principals." *Dissertation Abstracts International* 58(03A), 0664. University Microfilms No. 9726720.

Hammond, J., R. Keeney, and H. Raiffa. 2001. "Even Swaps: A Rational Method of Making Swaps." In *Harvard Business Review on Decision Making.* Boston: Harvard Business School Press. (Orig. pub. 1967.)

Hargrove, R. 1995. *Masterful Coaching: Extraordinary Results by Impacting People and the Way They Think and Work Together.* San Francisco: Jossey-Bass.

Hatano, G., and Y. Oura. 2003. "Commentary: Reconceptualizing School Learning Using Insight from Expertise Research." *Educational Researcher* 32 (8): 26–29.

Heath, S. 1983. *Ways with Words: Language, Life, and Work in Communities and Classrooms.* Cambridge: Cambridge University Press.

Henderson, A. T., and N. Berla. 1994. A New Generation of Evidence: The Family Is Critical to Student Achievement. St. Louis, MO: Danforth Foundation, and Flint, MI: Mott (C. S.) Foundation.

Institute for Educational Leadership. 2000. *Leadership for Student Learning: Reinventing the Principalship.* Washington, DC: Institute for Educational Leadership.

Jackson, P. 1995. *Sacred Hoops.* New York: Hyperion.

Keller, B. 1998. "Principal Matters." *Education Week.* November 11.

Kennedy, R. 1966. "Day of Affirmation." Speech, National Union of South African Students, Cape Town, South Africa, June 6.

Knowles, M., H. Elwood, and R. Swanson. 2005. *The Adult Learner.* San Diego, CA: Elsevier. (Orig. pub. 1973.)

Kouzes, J., and B. Posner. 1987. *Leadership Challenge: How to Get Extraordinary Things Done in Organizations.* San Francisco: Jossey-Bass.

Labaree, D. 1997. "Public Goods, Private Goods: American Struggle Over Educational Goals." *American Educational Research Journal* 34 (1): 39–81.

Labov, W. 1972. *Language in the Inner City: Studies in the Black English Vernacular.* Philadelphia: University of Pennsylvania Press.

Labov, W., and J. Waletzky. 1967. "Narrative Analysis: Oral Versions of Personal Experience." In *Analyzing Discourse: Text and Talk,* ed. J. Helm. Washington, DC: Georgetown University Press.

Lamb-Shapiro, J. 2005. "We Need Heart-Touching, Soul Penetrating Stories." *The Believer.* September.

Lashway, L., J. Mazarella, and T. Grundy. 1997. "Portrait of a Leader." In *School Leadership Handbook for Excellence,* 3rd ed., ed. S. C. Smith and P. L. Piele. Eugene, OR: ERIC Clearinghouse on Educational Management.

Lave, J., and E. Wenger. 1991. *Situated Learning: Legitimate Peripheral Participation.* Cambridge: University of Cambridge Press.

Lawrence-Lightfoot, S., and J. Hoffman Davis. 1997. *The Art and Science of Portraiture.* San Francisco: Jossey-Bass.

Leithwood, K., S. Anderson, and K. Wahlstrom. 2004. *How Leadership Influences Student Learning.* Minneapolis: University of Minnesota, and Toronto: University of Toronto.

Leithwood, K., and R. Steinbach. 1995. *Expert Problem Solving.* Albany: State University of New York Press.

Lewis, C. S. 1974. *Abolition of Man.* New ed., San Francisco: HarperOne.

Licata, J. W. 1978. "Consequence Analysis: Theory and Practice in School Problem Solving." *Educational Technology* 18 (9): 22–28.

Little, J. W. 2002. "Locating Learning in Teachers' Communities of Practice: Opening Up Problems of Analysis Records of Everyday Work." *Teaching and Teacher Education* 18: 917–946.

Lovely, S. 2006. *Setting Leadership Priorities*. Thousand Oaks, CA: Corwin.

Luthi, M. 1984. *The Fairytale's Art Form and Portrait of Man*. Bloomington, IN: University Press.

Macoby, M. 1976. "The Corporate Climber Has to Find His Heart." *Fortune*. October.

March, J. 1994. *A Primer on Decision Making: How Decisions Happen*. New York: The Free Press.

March, J., and J. Olsen. 1984. "The New Institutionalism: Organizational Factors in Political Life." *American Political Science Review* 78: 734–749.

March, J., and H. Simon. 1958. *Organizations*. New York: Wiley.

Marzano, R. 2003. *What Works in Schools: Translating Research into Action*. Alexandria, VA: Association for Supervision and Curriculum Development.

Maslow, A. H. 1943. "A Theory of Human Motivation." *Psychological Review* 50: 370–396.

Meyer, J., and B. Rowan. 1977. "Institutionalized Organizations: Formal Structure as Myth and Ceremony." *American Journal of Sociology* 83: 340–363.

Miles, M., and M. Huberman. 1996. *Qualitative Data Analysis*. Thousand Oaks, CA: Sage.

Mohrman, S., and E. Lawlor. 1996. "Motivation for School Reform." In *Rewards and Reform*, ed. S. Fuhrman and J. O'Day. San Francisco: Jossey-Bass.

Moore, D. 1999. *Where Have All the Principals Gone?* Rochester, MI: Oakland University.

Nelson, K., ed. 1989. *Narratives from the Crib*. Cambridge, MA: Harvard University Press.

Novak, J. 1998. *Learning, Creating, and Using Knowledge: Concept Maps as Facilitative Tools in Schools and Corporations.* Mahwah, NJ: Lawrence Erlbaum.

Ochs, E., and L. Capps. 2001. *Living Narrative: Creating Lives in Everyday Storytelling.* Cambridge, MA: Harvard University Press.

Ochs, E., and B. Schieffelin. 1989. "Language Has a Heart." Special issue, *The Pragmatics of Affect* 9 (1): 7–25.

Osterman, K., and R. Kottkamp. 1993. *Reflective Practice for Educators: Improving Schools Through Professional Development.* Newbury Park, CA: Corwin.

Palinscar, A. S., and A. I. Brown. 1984. "Reciprocal Teaching of Comprehension Fostering and Monitoring Activities." *Cognition and Instruction* I: 117–175.

Pavlenko, A. 2001. "Language Learning Memoirs as a Gendered Genre." *Applied Linguistics* 22 (2): 212–240.

Pepperl, J., and L. Lezotte. 2004. *What Effective Schools Research Says: Instructional Leadership.* Okemos, MI: Effective Schools Products.

Personal Narratives Group. 1989. *Interpreting Women's Lives: Feminist Theory and Personal Narratives.* Indianapolis: Indiana University Press.

Pfeffer, J. 1992. *Managing with Power: Politics and Influence in Organizations.* Boston: Harvard Business School Press.

Propp, V. I. 1958. *Morphology of the Fairytale.* Bloomington: Indiana University. (Orig. pub. 1928.)

Reason, P. 1988. *Human Inquiry in Action.* London: Sage.

Reeves, D. 2004. *Assessing Educational Leaders.* Thousand Oaks, CA: Corwin.

Roche, K. 1999. "Moral and Ethical Dilemmas in Catholic School Settings." In *Values and Educational Leadership*, ed. P. T Begley. Albany: State University of New York Press.

Rogers, C. R. 1969. *Freedom to Learn.* Columbus, OH: Merrill.

Rossiter, M. 1999. "A Narrative Approach to Development: Implications for Adult Education." *Adult Education Quarterly* 50 (1): 56–71.

Sage Learning Systems. 2001. "Facts and Figures from the Worlds of e-Learning, Training, Work, and Jobs." Sage Learning Systems. http://www.sagelearning.com/research_papers.htm.

Schön, D. A. 1983. *The Reflective Practitioner: How Professionals Think in Action.* San Francisco: Jossey-Bass.

———. 1987. *Educating the Reflective Practitioner: Toward a New Design for Teaching and Learning in the Professions.* San Francisco: Jossey-Bass.

Scott, R. 2003. *Organizations: Rational, Natural, and Open Systems.* Upper Saddle River, NJ: Prentice Hall.

Searle, J. 2004. *Mind: A Brief Introduction.* New York: Oxford University Press.

Senge, P. 1990. *The Fifth Discipline: The Art and Practice of the Learning Organization.* New York: Doubleday.

Senge, P., R. Ross, B. Smith, C. Roberts, and A. Kleiner. 1994. *The Fifth Discipline Fieldbook: Strategies and Tools for Building a Learning Organization.* New York: Doubleday.

Shaver, A., and R. Walls. 1998. "Effect of Title I Parent Involvement on Student Reading and Mathematics Achievement." *Journal of Research and Development in Education* 31: 90–97.

Simon, H. 1945. *Administrative Behavior.* New York: The Free Press.

Singleton, G., and C. Linton. 2006. *Courageous Conversations.* Thousand Oaks, CA: Corwin.

Smith, L., and P. Keith. 1971. *Anatomy of Educational Innovation: An Organizational Analysis of an Elementary School.* New York: John Wiley and Sons.

Smith, W., and R. Andrews. 1989. *Instructional Leadership: How Principals Make a Difference.* Alexandria, VA: Association for Supervision and Curriculum Development.

Sprague, N. 1973. "Involving the Assistant Principal on the Administrative Team." *National Association of Secondary School Principals Bulletin.* October.

Taylor, F. 1911. *The Principles of Scientific Management.* New York: Harper.

Tyack, D., and L. Cuban. 1995. *Tinkering Toward Utopia: A Century of Public School Reform.* Cambridge, MA: Harvard University Press.

Vygotsky, L. S. 1978. *Mind in Society: The Development of the Higher Psychological Processes.* Cambridge, MA: Harvard University Press.

Waters, T., and S. Kingston. 2005. "The Standards We Need." *Leadership* 35 (1): 14.

Waters, T., R. J. Marzano, and B. McNulty. 2003. *What 30 Years of Research Tells Us about the Effect of Leadership on Student Achievement.* Aurora, CO: McREL.

Weick, K. 1995. *Sensemaking in Organizations.* Thousand Oaks, CA: Sage.

West, C. 2001. *Race Matters.* Boston: Beacon.

Wheatly, M. 2002. *Turning to One Another: Simple Conversations to Restore Hope to the Future.* San Francisco: Berrett-Koehler.

Wheelis, A. 1973. *How People Change.* New York: Harper Torchbooks.

White, B. Y., and J. R. Fredrickson. 2000. "Metacognitive Facilitation: An Approach to Making Scientific Inquiry." In *Inquiring to Inquiry Learning and Teaching in Science*, ed. J. Minstrell and E. H. Van Zee. Washington, DC: American Association for the Advancement of Science.

Willower, D. 1994. "Dewey's Theory of Inquiry and Reflective Administration." *Journal of Educational Administration* 32 (1): 5–18.

Willower, D., and J. Licata. 1997. *Values and Valuation in the Practice of Educational Administration.* Thousand Oaks, CA: Corwin.

Wilshire, B. 1990. *The Moral Collapse of the University: Professionalism, Purity, and Alienation.* Albany: State University of New York Press.

Wilson, J. 1989. *Bureaucracy: What Government Agencies Do and Why They Do It.* New York: Basic Books.

Zimbardo, P. G. 1971. *The Power and Pathology of Imprisonment.* Congressional Record. (Serial No. 15, 1971-10-25). Hearings before Subcommittee No. 3, of the Committee on the Judiciary, House of Representatives, Ninety-Second Congress, First Session on Corrections, Part II, Prisons, Prison Reform and Prisoner's Rights: California. Washington, DC: U.S. Government Printing Office.

A

adult learning theory, 11–12
Anderson, S., 10
Argyris, C., 102
Aristotle, 119
Arum, R., 27
Assessing School Leaders (Reeves), 64–65

B

Ball, A., 100
Barnard, C., 101–102
Barth, R., 11, 64
Begley, P. T., 81
Bennis, W., 140, 149, 152
Berla, N., 83
biases, 52
Blankenstein, A., 13, 14, 145
Blasé, J., 82
Bloom, G., 133
Bolman, L. G., 100, 137
Bransford, J. D., 11
Bridges, E., 2
Brown, A. L., 11, 19
Bryk, A., 83

C

Campione, J. C., 11, 19
Carroll, L., 99
Caulfield, H., 140
Champy, J., 96
Cocking, R. R., 11
Cohen, M. D., 111
collaboration, 13
confluence, conflict or, 126–133
    institutional responsibilities and, 127
Courageous Conversations (Singleton), 52
Cuban, L., 14
    "Reforming Again and Again and Again," 85

D

Daley, B. J., 102
Davis, J. H., 6
Davis, K., 81
Deal, T. E., 100, 137
decision makers
    influences on, 86–87
    narratives and underlying influences on, 87–88
decision making
    components, 102–103
    flowchart, 114–116
decision-making influences, 82–84
    community members and, 83
    compendium of, 86–87
    parents and, 83
    students and, 82–83
    teachers and, 83
    upper-level administrators and, 84
decision-making influences, institutional
    district, state, and federal goals and, 85
    families and, 85
    fiscal concerns and, 85
    research and, 86
    role expectations and, 84–85
    school reform efforts and, 85–86
    values, guiding principles and, 86
Delpit, L., 39
DeMello, A., 9
Deutschman, A., 38
Drucker, P., 101
DuFour, R., 113
DuFour, R., R. Eaker, & R. Dufour, 12, 13, 15, 63

E

Eaker, R., 113
Elmore, R., 64
Emerson, Ralph Waldo, 96
emotional pincushions. *See* human pincushions
enforcers, 27–28
    reflective questions for, 36

enforcers-reflective storytelling
   aligning school policy, core values narrative, 30–32
   holding adults accountable narrative, 32–35
   switching roles, mid-performance narrative, 28–30
Epstein, J., 83
equity promoters, 51–53
   reflective questions for, 62
equity promoters-reflective storytelling
   damaging beautification narrative, 53–56
   power of the written word narrative, 56–57
   "vice principals' ghetto" narrative, 57–61
Etzioni, A., 88, 100–101

F

Ferguson, A., 52
Foucault, M., 28
Franklin, Benjamin, 101

G

Gandhi, Mahatma, 16
Gardner, H., 135
Goldsmith, J., 149, 152
Goleman, D., 18, 121
Gonzalez, D., 9

H

Hammond, J., 100, 101
Hatano, G., 102
Henderson, A. T., 83
hierarchy of needs, 14
Hoffman Davis, J., 151
human pincushions, 119–121
   awareness, lack thereof, narrative, 122–126
   confluence or conflict and, 126–133
   reflective questions for, 134

I

institutional responsibilities, 127
instructional leaders, 63–65
   reflective questions for, 78
instructional leaders-reflective storytelling
   arbitrary access to honors classes narrative, 68–71
   confinement of high standards narrative, 65–68
   issues with authority narrative, 74–77
   purple folders, black students narrative, 71–74

K

Keeney, R., 100, 101
Keith, P., 5
Kennedy, R., 46
Kottkamp, R., 17, 19
Kouzes, J., 138

L

Labaree, D., 85
Labov, W., 16, 105
Lao Tsu, *Tao Te Ching*, 141
Lave, J., 11
Lawlor, E., 76
Lawrence-Lightfoot, S., 5–6, 151
leaders, strong emotions and, 119–121
   See also human pincushions
Leadership Support Program (LSP), 2, 6–7
Leithwood, K., 10, 47, 102
Lewis, C. S., 96
Lezotte, L., 65
Licata, J., 81
Linton, C., 52, 60
Little, J. W., 22
Lovely, S., 143

M

March, J., 82, 84, 111
Maslow, A. H., 14, 47, 61, 77
metacognitive decision-making flowchart, 114–116

Metacognitive Decision-making Process Rubric, 102–103
Meyer, J., 14, 63
micropolitics, 82
Mohrman, S., 76
Moore, D., 10

N

narrative analysis, reflective storytelling process and, 22–23
narratives, professional learning and, 152
See also storytelling

O

Olsen, J., 84, 111
Osterman, K., 17, 19
Oura, Y., 102

P

Pepperl, J., 65
Posner, B., 138
principal decision makers, 99–103
   decision maker feelings of efficacy narrative, 112–114
   defined, 100
   reflective questions for, 117–118
   school rules, hungry parents narrative, 110–111
   student learning, internal angst narrative, 104–107
   student rights, teacher safety, versus narrative, 107–109
Principal Leadership Institute, 2
principals, roles of, 10
principalship, evolution of role of, 64–65
professional development, storytelling and, 19–20
professional learning communities
   role of, 13
   school leaders and, 14–15
Propp, V., 147

R

Raiffa, H., 100, 101
Reason, P., 1, 23, 119
Reeves, D., *Assessing School Leaders*, 64–65
reflective questions
   reflective storytelling process and, 24–25
reflective storytelling, 12–14
   narrative analysis and, 18
reflective storytelling process, 9, 20–22
   changes in practice and the, 23
   narrative analysis and, 22–23
   prompts for, 21
   reflective questions and, 22
   See also storytelling
"Reforming Again and Again and Again" (Cuban), 85
Roche, K., 119
Rowan, B., 14, 63

S

Schon, D. A., 1, 100, 153
school leaders, 5–8
   critical role of, 9–11
   defining success in growth, novice to expert narrative, 143–145
   inhabiting role of, 135–136
   Leadership Support Program (LSP), 6–7
   lessons for new leaders narrative, 145–146
   magical objects narrative, 147–149
   meaningful-making narrative, 140–141
   professional learning communities and, 14–15
   reflective questions for, 150
   roles of, 5–6
   sense-making, ambiguity narrative, 137–139
   tensions in school leadership narrative, 141–143
   See also enforcers; equity promoters; instructional leaders; system builders
school leadership, decisions, values, emotions and, 79–80
Searle, J., 17
Senge, P., 39
Shaver, A., 83
Simon, H., 82, 102, 113

Singleton, G., 60
 Courageous Conversations, 52
Smith, D., 17
Smith, L., 5
Sprague, N., 39
Steinbach, R., 47, 102
storytelling, 2–3
 power of, 16–17, 151–152
 professional development and, 19–20
 professional learning and, 152
 theory development and, 17–19
 See also reflective storytelling process
system builders, 37–38
 attitudes, beliefs and, 39
 collaboration and, 39–40
 reflective questions for, 48–49
 systems, structures and, 38
system builders–reflective storytelling
 calculating how hard to push narrative, 40–42
 guiding teams past administrative roadblocks
  narrative, 44–47
 scorching bridges for a clean school narrative,
  42–44

T

Tao Te Ching (Lao Tsu), 141
theory development, storytelling and, 17–19
Tyack, D., 14

V

values, 81–82
 authenticity over outcomes narrative, 91–93
 outcomes and avoidance narrative, 93–96
 reflective questions for, 97
 truth of harmony narrative, 88–90

W

Wahlstrom, K., 10
Waletzky, J., 16
Wallace Foundation Report, 10

Walls, R., 83
Waltetzky, J., 105
Wenger, E., 11
Willower, D., 81
Wilson, J., 102

Z

Zimbardo, P. G., 28